Living on the Water

Living on the Water

Elizabeth McMillian

RIZZOLI
NEW YORK

First published in the United States of America in 1998 by
RIZZOLI INTERNATIONAL PUBLICATIONS, INC.
300 Park Avenue South, New York, New York 10010
Reprinted in paperback, 2002

ISBN 0-8478-2445-4 paperback
ISBN 0-8478-2115-3 hardcover
LC 98-65890

Printed in Singapore

half-title page Fallingwater by
Frank Lloyd Wright, Pennsylvania
title page Villa of Water by Kengo Kuma,
Shizuoka, Japan

Contents

Introduction

Whether focusing on a distant line where land meets the infinite ocean horizon via a rocky cliff – or sprawling towards the peaceful edge of a nearby canal, lake or pond – or perching directly above the pounding surf or a quiet spring ... houses built near the water capture that element's sensual poetics. Our world provides many evocative watery settings – oceans and seas, bays and harbours, creeks and canals, natural grottoes and waterfalls – and, like human beings since the dawn of time, we continue to gravitate towards sites like these for the beauty and experience of nature that they provide.

A constant awareness of water is the key experience to be achieved by any successful house designed near it. Whether one defines the experience of water in hedonistic, intellectual, spiritual or mystical terms, the elements of sight, sound, smell, humidity and wind lead to expanded human consciousness. A number of planning and building elements can enhance the magic of such awareness: the amount of glazing and anchoring to the site, pathways and access to the water, terraces and patios, lines of sight, directions of sunrise and sunset. Since humidity and wind take their toll on materials and structure, and since sound, sun and water itself take their

above On the island of Capri off Italy's Tyrrhenian coast Curzio Malaparte built his starkly modern writer's retreat in 1939. The stone house is topped by an unprotected roof terrace reached by a wedge-shaped stair.

right A suspension bridge links Casa Mi Ojo to a peninsula at Costa Careyes, Mexico. The house was designed by Marco Aldaco, Alberto Mazzoni and Gianfranco Brignone.

toll on human comfort, finding the right combination of sensual enjoyment and elemental control is the architect's task. The interface between traditional, low-tech, environmentally friendly solutions and state-of-the-art methods and materials provides for the most interesting results in terms of both comfort and unique building forms.

At the global level, collective consciousness and regional wisdom together have informed cultural traditions, local building practices and even social customs which enhance the craft of living on the water. Among renowned waterside locations, there are Venice, with its canals and Carnival; Paris, with the Rive Gauche and café society; the Hudson River Valley in New York State, with its folksy legends of Sleepy Hollow and its early twentieth-century decor and social mores so tellingly documented by Edith Wharton. In China and Japan, locations near water house the spirit of water. Canals and bays have both practical and spiritual significance; ponds and lakes, traditionally the locations of palaces and temples, are settings for everyone to visit in order to claim a bit of heaven. Oriental houses, inspired by long tradition, use water symbolically to separate the spiritual from the material world.

Water, Culture and Meaning

Every culture assigns its own meanings to water and has its own way of thinking about it metaphorically and building in relation to it. Most cultures, however, hold in common a cluster of overlapping mythical and metaphorical interpretations that underscores the universal character of water.

One of these is the concept of representing nature in terms of elemental symbolism, with deep water representing the Abyss, and the horizon representing Infinity. Another is the identification of water with purification that leads to spiritual rejuvenation. A further cluster of meanings involves the therapeutic effects of water that promise health and beauty and gave rise to the mythical Fountain of Youth. Allied to this is the concept of water as a symbol of fertility and reproduction. In all world religions, water is a source and symbol of life, yet several faiths also reveal its destructive side as a force which can bring about death and ruin through floods and storms.

Aside from myth, metaphor and geomorphic aesthetics, it was the practical invention of nautical crafts and the engineering of harbours that led human beings to challenge the vast power and dominion of the sea. In so doing, fishing, trade and defense became the three potent needs which brought urban structures to the water's edge, thereby causing – or inspiring – dwellings both fashionable and practical to spring up there.

Western Traditions

In ancient Greece, springs and groves were dedicated to the gods and ornamented as sacred shrines. Thus, natural bodies of water took on spiritual meaning, and the existing topography and scenery influenced the landscaping and siting of buildings. The earliest residential gardens were also influenced by expeditions to Persia, where the Greeks encountered *parridaeza,* large enclosures surrounded by pools and landscaped with flowers, trees and aromatic shrubs. Elaborating on their own conceptions of the significance of water in the landscape, the Greeks developed pavilions, grottoes and nymphaea watered by fountains or springs and shaded by porticos and tree-lined walks. These served gymnasiums, centres for philosophical instruction and discussion.

Following the reign of Alexander the Great, Greek culture spread throughout the Mediterranean basin, and modified versions of Classical villas, orientated towards the sea and embellished with water gardens, appeared in Asia Minor, North Africa and other colonial outposts. Using Vitruvius's writings on Hellenistic pleasure gardens, the ancient Romans designed porticoed villas or pavilions, sited like remote temples on rocky promontories overlooking the sea. Seaside and lakeside topography inspired imaginative planning to gain the advantages of scenic views, morning sun and protective moorings. Terraced gardens, carefully sited dining spaces, bathing pools, constructed walks, colonnades and porticos were organized with particular attention to the natural setting.

The interest in natural waterscapes led to the construction of large Roman Imperial estates and gardens at lake- and seaside locations. Examples include Nero's Golden House, a first-century-AD villa compound designed by Lucullus, and the villa built by the Emperor

Hadrian at Tivoli between 118 and 138 AD. Hadrian had a marble island constructed within his compound as a haven to which he could escape from the pressures of overseeing his growing empire. This island, called the Maritime Theatre because of the mock naval skirmishes staged in the moat surrounding it, originally could be accessed only by two wooden swing-bridges. It had dining-rooms, a small library and a central fountain enclosed by intricate colonnading.

From the fall of Rome in the fifth century to the time of the Crusades, Byzantium (now Istanbul) was the great trading centre of the Mediterranean. Like the Italian medieval ports of Venice, Genoa and Pisa, Byzantium was a fortified harbour town. Towers and protective walls struck looming poses in counterpoint to the horizontal infinity of the sea and harbour. In Britain, waterside fortresses were known as bastides, while in Scandinavia, the land-side sections of similar structures were protected by moats and drawbridges. A similar contrapuntal feeling is still evoked by Mont-St-Michel, the thirteenth-century refuge for Benedictine monks which rises out of the Atlantic off the Normandy coast of France. Not a port structure or fortified castle, but rather a medieval compound which appears to be carved out of the natural stone outcropping, Mont-St-Michel is a fusion of architecture and island.

Classically Inspired Water Gardens

Water, shaped by Classical principles of symmetry and geometry and animated by skilful hydraulics developed by the ancient Greeks and Romans, became an intrinsic part of Renaissance and, most particularly, Baroque residential architecture. Jets, fountains, cascades and decorative sculptural compositions embodied the Baroque fascination with movement and infinite space. The best of the Baroque spirit is expressed in such Italian gardens as the Ville d'Este at Tivoli outside Florence. Monumental cascades grace the Palazzo Reale at Caserta, as well as other grand estates of Europe, such as the Wilhelmshohe Castle at Kassel in Germany, Chatsworth in England and many of the French châteaux in the countryside around Paris and on the River Loire. In Louis XIV's palaces and parks, with their distinctive axial plans by André Le Nôtre, water was also used as a decorative and visually dominant feature. Existing inlets and lakes were incorporated into the unified landscapes of the palaces of Fontainebleau, Versailles and Vaux-le-Vicomte. Today, the Baroque water garden is thought of as an extension of monumental architecture and an environment for courtly entertainment.

Adeptly developed in the sixteenth and seventeenth centuries, devices such as pressurized water, water organs, spraying fountains and cascades mimic and manipulate the effects of natural bodies of water. Their distinction is that they are human inventions, imitations of natural phenomena. Such fanciful features are ultimately among the greatest landscaping contributions of the ancient Greeks and Romans, who recognized the social and therapeutic qualities of water, offering aqueducts, public baths and drinking fountains to citizens and colonial subjects alike.

The Canal Houses of Amsterdam and Venice

Maritime transportation, trade and naval activity expanded in many countries between the fourteenth and seventeenth centuries. A network of prominent port cities grew along the principal navigable rivers of Italy, Flanders, Germany and France, and along the Baltic, the North Sea and the Mediterranean, with the construction or implementation of quays, wharves, harbours, arsenals, docks and fortifications. Holland and Flanders in particular enlarged their ports, transforming them into total urban environments with the expansion of canal systems in such cities as Amsterdam and Bruges.

The practical Dutch developed a system of dykes to control the flow of water, reclaim land and improve trade. In Amsterdam's 'golden age' – the seventeenth century – the city was divided into urban and residential zones by an arrangement of parallel canals intersected by narrow lanes. Building ordinances strictly controlled architectural cohesion, and the canal houses built by citizen-merchants were modest in size. In many cases, a commercial warehouse would be accommodated in the same building as a private residence. Traditionally, the cold climate permitted only small- and medium-sized windows, and, only rarely, a balcony or loggia might open on to the canal. In modern times, climate-control systems made it possible for the Dutch to open up their houses with large sheets of glass to enjoy water views.

Unlike the residences of Dutch canal cities, those of

Representative of early riverside
settlements throughout the
world, Philipsburg Manor and
Grist-mill, with its picturesque
paddle-wheel and millpond
bridge at North Tarrytown, New
York, was begun in 1693 by
Dutchman Frederick Philipse.
Located where the Pocantico
and Hudson rivers meet, the
hipped-roof stone manor house
in Catskill-Adirondack style was
doubled in size by Adolphus
Philipse. The early eighteenth-
century wood-frame grist-mill
is considered one of the finest
early industrial buildings.

Sunnyside At the Gothicized,
stepped-gable entrance of
Washington Irving's Sunnyside,
wisteria frames a view of the
Hudson River at a historic
section, known as the Tappan
Zee. Dormers, chimney-pots and
large windows accent the one-
and-a-half-storey seventeenth-
century cottage, enlarged and
remodelled by Irving in 1835.
The house is a cluster of red-
shingled structures, including a
curved-roof 'Spanish' tower
influenced by Irving's travels as
an internationally known author
and diplomat.

Venice reflect the various levels of local society and
provide a unique record of residential canal architecture,
displaying a panoply of Byzantine, Gothic, Renaissance
and Baroque styles. The lagoon location is at the outflow
of two rivers from Lombardy into the Adriatic Sea.
Residences are found along both of the major canals,
which follow the original river-beds, and the network of
minor canals, as well as 'inland', where houses face small
civic spaces (*campi*), pedestrian streets and alleyways
(*calli*). As in Holland, the original river-facing *casa
fondago* started as a combination of residence and
warehouse for trading. The *casa*s were replaced by the
palaces of successful merchant-princes, for whom the
Grand Canal was the favoured location. Unlike Dutch
canal-side houses and fortified palaces in other parts of
Italy, Venetian palaces of two to four storeys open on to
the canals with windows, doors, loggias and porticoed
loading docks. The canals themselves were crossed by
numerous picturesque bridges, and the Neoclassical
renovations of the late eighteenth and nineteenth
centuries gave the city the appearance and scale it
retains today.

Houses along the Hudson River

Following the completion of the Erie Canal in 1825,
the American state of New York experienced an influx
of tens of millions of people from neighbouring states
and other countries. The cities of Rochester, Syracuse,
Utica and Buffalo grew from frontier villages, and
the valleys of the Hudson and Mohawk rivers (water
highways to the West) experienced the heaviest
migration in American history.

Members of the upper class settled in the Hudson
River Valley, where they built stylish residences with
views of the water. The notion of practicality governed
the straightforward design of one of the river's earliest
'manor' houses, the Philipsburg Manor. Frederick
Philipse built both a stone house and a grist-mill
immediately at the river's edge in what is now North
Tarrytown. In 1720, his son Adolphus Philipse doubled
the size of the original house to its present dimensions.
The clapboard mill and simple, whitewashed house are
typical of the Catskill-Adirondack vernacular.

An interest in style became more pronounced in the
next century, when the Palladian-influenced plantation
houses of the American South were copied in the

North along the Hudson, notably at Edgewater, a
grand house built in 1820. Soon, however, white temple-
like structures gave way to Gothic Revival 'villas'.
Washington Irving, the American master of folklore and
fiction, history and biography, had his seventeenth-
century cottage remodelled in Gothic style in 1835.
Called Sunnyside, the house partakes of an unspoilt
setting only feet away from the Hudson on a section of
the river known as the Tappan Zee. The author of *The
Legend of Sleepy Hollow* and *Rip Van Winkle* must have
taken delight in the medieval revival style and its fanciful
allusions to the house's wooded setting.

Oriental, Islamic and European elements were
combined in a grandiose Victorian manner for the 1874
Hudson River hilltop villa of landscape artist Frederick
Edwin Church. Travelling to such remote corners of the
earth as the Arctic Circle and the Andes, Church
portrayed exotic landscapes in his hugely successful
paintings. He enjoyed the professional guidance of
Calvert Vaux and Frederick Law Olmsted, leading
American landscape architects of the time, but acted as
his own architect and decorator for the house, which he
called Olana, combining ornamental forms and motifs
from foreign lands and distant ages. Olana's towers,
porches and gazebos offer some of the most romantically
framed views of the Hudson.

Colonial Ports

In recent centuries, the establishment of colonial port
cities at locations such as Cape Town, Hong Kong, Rio
de Janeiro, Buenos Aires and Bombay helped to spread
design ideas from Western Europe to waterside
residential developments throughout the world. The
quality of the relationship between residential port
development and the relevant body of water depended
on the beauty of the topography – as at Rio de Janeiro
and San Francisco – or on the wealth of the port – as at
Monaco and Hong Kong – or, finally, on the beauty of
local traditions – as in Indonesia and the Caribbean.

By the end of the seventeenth century, Spanish,
French, English, Dutch and Swedish colonizers had
established port cities characterized by their particular
cultural forms. In New England, colonists established
farms and plantations along the waterways of the original
Virginia colony at Jamestown. Classical Palladian designs
– inspired by the fashions of England and France – were

adopted by prominent families wishing to establish solid traditions of their own in the New World. Both George Washington's Mt Vernon and Thomas Jefferson's Monticello are hilltop Palladian houses with expanses of land leading to river views. It was this arcadian tradition, evoked initially by Washington and formalized by Jefferson, which led to the colonnaded-porch-and-temple-pediment formula of the grand Mississippi River plantations.

The large settlements of Boston Bay in Massachusetts and Manhattan Island in New York, with their waterfronts, wharves and piers, provided the opportunity for merchants and tradespeople to become urban dwellers with waterside houses. The island of Manhattan, located between the Hudson and East rivers and touching the Atlantic Ocean, grew from the early seventeenth century. The city of Chicago, located in Illinois on Lake Michigan at the mouth of the Chicago River, developed as a natural transhipment centre for the American Middle West in the nineteenth century. In 1830, the construction of a canal linking the Great Lakes with the Mississippi River conceptually joined up the pragmatic plains of the Middle West with the arcadian and Neoclassical South. That Chicago subsequently embraced modernism is illustrated by the waterside housing of Mies van der Rohe's Lake Shore Drive Apartments and the Marina City development, which includes apartments, offices, shops and docking facilities for boats. Outside Chicago, the Great Lakes region is rich in both regional and international modern residential expressions. Frank Lloyd Wright's own retreat and school at Spring Green, Wisconsin, is just one of many modern masterworks built as riverside or lake-side vacation retreats in the area.

The oldest North American colonial port city is St Augustine, Florida, a typical sixteenth-century Spanish colonial town established between 1565 and 1821. Its original residences opened loggias and arcades on to the coastal setting. However, the port was not as successful as had been hoped, and waterside housing there never achieved architectural richness. San Francisco, by contrast, has made the most of its port-city birthright. Founded in 1776, the protected harbour city benefitted economically from the mid-nineteenth-century Gold Rush and the completion of the Transcontinental Railroad in 1896. Additionally, fishing, shipbuilding and

manufacturing turned the city into a major port. Rebuilding after the 1906 earthquake and fire increased awareness of – and code protection for – the significant aesthetic qualities of water, topography, view and historic maritime character. Zoning provisions insist upon low height for structures located near the waterfront, establish viewing corridors and retain significant historic buildings. Thus, urban hillside homes have bay vistas and enjoy views of the Golden Gate Bridge, Sausalito Island or restaurants and tourist attractions such as Fish Alley, the inner lagoons of Fisherman's Wharf, or Black Point Cove and North Beach.

Despite the beauty of these urban harbour views, many San Franciscans – like the inhabitants of Cannes, Venice and other fashionable port cities – have weekend retreats nearby where they can enjoy the same water views in unobstructed natural settings. Near San Francisco, residents opt for one of the small, spread-out residential communities of Carmel, Pebble Beach, Big Sur or Sea Ranch, with their craggy Northern California coastal terrain. From the unique woodsy houses there, which have become the trademark vernacular of the area, one can partake more serenely of the watery environment.

Eastern Traditions

The Islamic World

An Islamic city's water supply represented both its wealth and its spiritual strength. Like the ancient Greeks and Romans, Muslim garden designers manipulated water to create fountains, cascades, channels and pools, providing dynamic and tranquil visual effects. The *hamman*, or water garden, was modelled on Classical thermae with their water displays, fountains and basins. However, the *hamman* excluded the areas for physical activity which were common to the Roman prototype. Though a public space, the *hamman* was intended to be a place for contemplation, meditation and pleasure like the residential or palace garden.

The gardens of pre-Islamic Persia, which used water for irrigation, display and sound effects, influenced early Muslim garden designs in the Near East. The concept of a private enclosed or walled garden with springs and fountains imitating a view of Paradise – the Persian

Sea Ranch Mr and Mrs James Alinder's house at Sea Ranch in northern California enjoys both the Pacific Ocean and a rushing stream. Its outlines are those of simple rural shed roofs based on barns dating from the ranch's agricultural past. Building materials naturally blend with the gray and brown rocks and golden grasses, including thick posts, coppery green trim and rusting metal nails, undecorated windows and steps made of railroad ties and grass treads. Strong winds and a rolling California landscape of beaches amid deep coves, cliffs, and inland hills characterize the northern California coast where the Sea Ranch homes and condominiums were built in the mid-1960s. Created by Moore, Lyndon, Turnbull, Whitaker with landscape architect Lawrence Halprin, Sea Ranch expresses a model coastal community in harmony with the landscape of trees, views, paths and meadows, and with regional design and environmental concerns.

parridaeza – suited the Islamic notion of water as the source of life, providing spiritual meaning as well as an essential amenity in an arid climate. Sites were chosen and arranged by geomantic means. The basic garden courtyard was an enclosed quadrangle, divided into four sections by water channels symbolizing four rivers branching from a common source and dividing the earth.

From the eighth to the fifteenth centuries, southern Spain was occupied by Muslim colonizers, and a wealth of residential structures from that period include Islamic water gardens. The best-known examples are at Granada. The first to be built in what is now a complex of palaces was the Alhambra, constructed in 1238 as a fortress in the Sierra Nevada. The River Darro was channelled into reservoirs to serve the complex in the fourteenth century, when a group of Nasrid palaces was built in what is now the middle of the complex. These palaces comprise series of pavilions and arcaded courtyards which display the essential character of the Islamic water garden to its best advantage. The courtyards present highly ornate surfaces, sounds, reflections and light patterns conveying associations with fresh water. The Court of Lions has surrounding arcades, a pavilion at each side and a central basin supported by twelve sculpted lions. Water channels extend from the centre of the court to the surrounding pavilions, where slender columns and arcading form a delicate screen. Darro River water also activates the fountains, pools, jets and water sprays of the adjacent summer palace of the sultans of Granada, the Generalife. Pavilions and open

Classical-style peristyles interweave with water channels and fountains there. The Generalife inspired such modern environments as fashion designer Yves St Laurent's Majorelle water garden and house at Marakesh in North Africa.

India and the Water Gardens of Kashmir and Srinigar

The River Ganges has a sacred role in Hindu religion. Steps called *ghat*s lead down to the water, tying together sacred temples and people's everyday acts of purification. Pools for bathing were also constructed within temples. In addition to the sacred Ganges, grotto-like wells are also of religious significance, and sites with a nearby natural source of water are considered sacred. Thus Hindu temples are often sited on rivers, streams or ponds.

During the Mughal Empire, the influence of Persian-style pleasure gardens reached northern India. The public lake-side water gardens in the Vale of Kashmir at Lake Dal and at the capital of Srinagar incorporate water from tank reservoirs. The series of courtyards and terraces channel water to various levels over sloping, textured chutes, called *chador*s, to form cascades, and lead to geometric pools and fountains. Water is channelled through pavilions sited to overlook the water gardens and the countryside. The enclosing low walls permit a visual link to the surrounding view.

Elaborate water gardens were often part of Indian palace design. In the capital city of Delhi, the Mughal Red Fort was originally designed as a water palace,

Lake Palace Reached by boat, Jag Mandir, the Lake Palace at Udaipur, is set in the middle of Pichola Lake in northern India. The main façade consists of a central projection with three fanciful domed belvederes. Around the sides, domed arcades and galleries are built out over the water. Arising directly out of the lake, the two-storey white stone compound seems twice as tall reflected in the water. The Mughal-influenced Hindu structure was originally built in the late seventeenth century by a young prince for romantic trysts. It is owned by the Maharana of Udaipur and leased to the Taj Hotel group as Lake Palace Hotel.

where water from the Ganges fed the fountains, cascades, waterfalls and water channels within the private apartments. The Jag Mandir, an island palace at Udaipur, now serves as a hotel where arcades and galleries extend over the water. Less affluent residents of Kashmir enjoy simpler designs at Lake Dal and along the Srinigar coast, where wooden houseboats are a common residential form.

Chinese and Japanese Traditions

At the basis of all Chinese design is the notion that spirit and matter co-exist as equals, thus making possible tranquility and oneness with nature. Early Japanese religion likewise emphasized the forces of nature. The T'ang Dynasty in China, in particular, inspired Japanese gardeners to separate the spiritual from the material world symbolically by using water. Japanese gardens provide a retreat for leisure and meditation on nature. During the Heian (Kyoto) period, natural elements such as tree-covered mountains with springs, streams and rivers were studied, conventionalized and reconstructed in gardens as hills, rocks, ponds and cascades interspersed with bridges, pavilions, pagodas and shrines. Likewise, seascape elements were reproduced in gardens with spring-fed ponds or lakes bordered by rocks and boulders, thus creating a variety of inlets and promontories. Later, Zen meditation gardens were conceived in the same manner, with stones symbolizing – and representing the spiritual essence of – waterfalls, bridges and islands, and sand representing water.

One special way to introduce water into Oriental houses is the *torii* (gateway), traditionally used to define the entrance to a sacred temple. The ritual of stepping through the gateway represents the transition from the profane to the sacred. A spectacular use of the *torii* is seen in the bay surrounding the Japanese island of Miyajima, where such a gateway has recently been placed in the water. Cross-beams frame the inland mountains from one side and the bay from the other, thus transforming the sea into a temple of nature.

Resorts and Waterside Communities

If awareness of the water itself is the design ingredient intrinsic to the siting of a house by the water's edge, then the second most important ingredient is the ability of the waterside house to refresh. Resorts, so attractive to holiday-makers, are located near lakes and oceans for just this reason. The well-travelled are familiar with the long list of beautiful locations on islands and along oceans. Lakes also draw their share of visitors in search of tranquility, and rivers provide pleasant destinations for those wishing to escape from urban pressures.

In the early eighteenth century, the European seaside became popular for its curative waters. In England, the quaint and picturesque character of quiet fishing villages appealed to a growing number of urban dwellers who longed for pastoral simplicity. During the nineteenth century, British resorts such as Brighton began to mushroom, while in America, new wealth was used to build resorts, in particular enormous single-family homes in New England. At Newport, Rhode Island, and in Massachusetts, Connecticut and Maine at Nantucket, Martha's Vineyard, Hyannis Port and Mystic, Americans built seaside houses, first employing the Georgian style from Britain and then creating their own individual variants. Practitioners of one of these variants, the Shingle Style, used natural wood shingles and local stone to blend into the setting. To this day, architects and designers are inspired by these regional variations and reproduce them in highly disciplined, traditional ways or more playfully, incorporating contemporary design interests and new ways to approach the water.

The residential development of Newport, Rhode Island, was exceptional in American architectural history. In the late nineteenth century, this resort for the wealthy saw the construction of numerous grand mansions at the seaside which have no peers anywhere in the world. The best example is The Breakers, a formal mansion with a sweeping view of the water designed by the most prestigious architect of America's Gilded Age, Richard Morris Hunt, for Cornelius Vanderbilt III. Hunt based his design, with its extensive loggias, arcades and terraces, on sixteenth-century palazzi at Genoa and Turin. The grounds include a three-mile paved trail along the ocean, called Cliff Walk.

Florida also had its grand resorts during the early twentieth century. Viscaya, on Biscayne Bay, has been described as a '70-room Mediterranean Xanadu'. Completed in 1914 for the wealthy Chicago industrialist James Deering, this elaborate structure embraces the bay, creating a relationship between house and water which was rare in Florida at the time. Inspired by Italian villas, particularly the seventeenth-century Venetian Palazzo Rezzonico, Viscaya was constructed of reinforced concrete and stucco with local oolitic limestone trim and Florida quarry steps incorporating coral formations. Deering protected his two yachts against the tides with a breakwater in the form of a 176-foot stone barge reminiscent of the Barcaccia in Rome or the stone junk in Beijing. The landscaping of the 180-acre estate includes formal gardens and stepped pavilions mimicking the Villa d'Este in Tivoli and the Villa Albani in Rome, a three-hundred-foot-long sea-wall, a domed pavilion and a gondola canal with a footbridge.

Camps and lodges offer a way to escape to a groomed and lavishly serviced version of the wilderness along inland waters around the world. Many nineteenth- and twentieth-century resorts can be found at such locations as Lake Maggiore and Lake Geneva and along the Loire and Danube rivers. Across America there are camps along lakes and rivers established by the forestry and park services. Whilst historic traditions for refined-masonry hunting lodges exist, lodges of logs and timber located along streams and lake shores throughout Bavaria and Scandinavia may have inspired the popular American Adirondack Style, although these days the style claims the crude huts of early American settlers as its roots.

The Adirondack wilderness of New York State was opened up for tourism with the completion of Thomas Durant's Adirondack Railroad in 1871. Durant's son William established towns and promoted the region for resort living, beginning in 1879 with the summer retreat of Camp Pine Knot, located on a peninsula projecting into Raquette Lake. Employing log construction, unpeeled limbs and branches of cedar and spruce for ornamental porch railings and gable screens, the rustic aesthetic was continued in the interiors with massive local stone fireplaces and birch-bark wall and ceiling coverings. For a year-round house, William Durant built the three-and-a-half-storey Sagamore Lodge on the shores of Shedd Lake (renamed Sagamore Lake). The size and grandeur of this log house set new standards for camp-style living and drew the attention of America's Gilded Age families. Alfred Gwynne Vanderbilt bought Sagamore Lodge

in 1901 and expanded the compound even further.

Vanderbilt's architectural stamp can best be seen at Kamp Kill Kare on Lake Kora, where he hired renowned architect John Russell Pope to design a monumental log house in 1913. The main lodge, which descends the sloping terrain to the lakeshore, is made up of separate split-log buildings linked to form a multilevelled, gabled, dormered and verandaed structure more than three hundred feet long. Although the Pope design is a rustic masterpiece, untrained local builder Ben Muncil, Jr's design for Topridge is considered the best example of the Adirondack Style. Built on St Regis Lake for heiress Marjorie Merriweather Post, the sixty-eight-building complex has a multilevelled rough wood exterior. The main living-room is eighty feet long with thirty-foot timber beams, and its trusses are hung with grand antler chandeliers and Native American kayaks, subtle reminders of its location near water.

Millionaire industrialists like the Vanderbilts had an impact far beyond the territory of regional vacation homes. Along with nineteenth-century advances in technology and economic changes, they affected residential water settings around the world. While seventeenth- and eighteenth-century port cities drew resort activities, the next century saw a change in scale which made water access increasingly difficult. On some international coasts, the relationship between community life and the waterway was changed forever as passenger transport and import and export business increased. Larger ships, maintenance docks and waterfront structures were needed to provide storage, supplementary industries, processing and maintenance for ports. These needs created large industrial zones with roads and railways which separated towns and waterfronts. A prime example is the quaint city of Rotterdam, with a port situated on the Rhine/Maas delta. Currently the second-largest city of the Netherlands, Rotterdam prospered throughout the last two centuries and, when it built Europort in 1958, became the largest port city in the world. Although master planners showed particular consideration for the environmental qualities of the river delta and included extensive leisure and conservation areas, they nonetheless crowded out resort and residential development.

In the years following World War II, existing seaside

Viscaya American Gilded Age resort architecture came to Florida when, in the early decades of the twentieth century, the wealthy Chicago industrialist James Deering built Viscaya on Biscayne Bay. The elaborate 'baroque' structure, completed in 1914, was designed by F. Burral Hoffman and inspired in part by the seventeenth-century Venetian Palazzo Rezzonico. It is trimmed with local oolitic limestone and quarry stones. Viscaya is maintained as a public house-museum and park.

towns responded to the new demands for resorts and the trend towards outdoor recreation and entertainment. Cliff-like seashore hotels and flats were built in cities such as Miami, Florida, and Palma, Majorca. After the 1950s, planners on the Roussillon-Languedoc coast of France learned from earlier mistakes and established a new format for seaside resort villages and marina communities, factoring certain environmental considerations into their schemes. Analyzing tide conditions, prevailing winds, wave characteristics and drift with safe access for pleasure craft as well as beach sports in mind, they designed contemporary structures with architectural interest as well as practical vehicular access and parking to create a small, traditional harbour town. Similar projects were built at Baie des Anges, near Nice, at La Grande Motte and at Port Grimaud. In Mexico, similar marina complexes, often run by hotel chains, provide connected villas at Cancun, Las Hadas and Careyes. The diversity of architectural expression in the new resorts and waterside structures ranges from historical and regional vernacular to the rational lines of modernism.

Some modern residential waterside communities looked to the past for timeless planning elements. Seaside, developed in the late 1970s, is an eighty-acre resort community located in the Florida panhandle with a half-mile of beach fronting the Gulf of Mexico. The master planners, Andres Duany and Elizabeth Plater-Zyberk, designed the community to maximize variety in land use, building types and architectural styles. While not every house has a close relationship to the gulf, every resident has access to the beach through the use of delightful Neoclassical waterfront pavilions. In the 1950s, residential scale was also the winning factor in the successful development of the Club Mediterranée villages, which adopted the Polynesian camp with grass huts and other tropical and subtropical forms from countries such as Malaysia and the Philippines as inspiration for resorts. Unique regional waters provided the themes for each location, as at the Club Med at Sebatu in Bali, where natural baths bubble up from volcanic arteries and fountains spill into a series of deep bathing pits surrounded by lush palm canopies.

Whether exotic or familiar, contemporary houses by the water's edge have been inspired by elements of resort design. Bridges, pavilions, gardens, pleasure piers, stone-lined natural pools and a gamut of regional traditions and historic allusions have combined with modern ingenuity to create waterside homes imbued with a sense of refreshment and delight, while providing a constant reminder of the crucial importance of water.

By the Sea

'Living on the edge', a common way of describing a daring life style, has often been associated with a psychological orientation towards the edges of continents. The horizon – that vision of infinity – represents freedom. Additionally, a preference for a coastal setting represents a psychological connection to the planet's Ocean. Made up of actual oceans, seas, rivers, lakes, ice and ground-water, the Ocean – known also as the hydrosphere – comprises seventy-one per cent of the earth's surface. Every drop of seawater reminds us that it is part of an ongoing cycle of global exchange, belonging to no specific time or place. Through careful siting, waterside houses create personal places connected to the cycle of the world's Ocean.

Oceans and seas absorb water from rain, rivers and streams and lose water by evaporation from their enormous surfaces. Their huge volumes of water move within themselves. Internal waves have maximum strength at depth, while most surface waves are strengthened by wind and continue on as swell. Travelling towards the shore, waves run into shallow water, where their height increases; finally, they become narrower and steeper to form breakers or surf. Water surging forwards and flowing back on itself in constantly changing, mesmerizing rhythms provides both a visual feast and a repertoire of soothing and exciting natural sounds. These tidal waves – gravity waves determined by the relative positions of the moon, earth and sun – provide the most striking impression of the power of the sea. The term 'tide' is also used in a looser sense to refer to surges, storm tides and other meteorological events, since the seasons, coastal geography and atmospheric conditions all affect wave action. Although tidal forces are minimal in comparison with the earth's gravitational forces, their effects can be considerable.

Waves, strong ocean winds and dramatic views of the horizon characterize seaside residential communities with their typical piers and lighthouses. Piers extend out into navigable oceans as landing places and promenades or simply to protect and form harbours; they are accessible public spaces. Coastal lighthouses, by contrast, suggest the hermit's existence. Their unique vertical shapes are recognizable anywhere in the world. Usually plastered in white but often painted with stripes and patterns so that sailors can identify their positions during daylight hours, lighthouses have simple, handsome detailing which is also understated so as not to compete with the pristine landscape of coast and ocean. Subject to the physical challenges of living by the water, they are laid out to resist wind and sea alike and bear witness to the drama and excitement of ocean-side locations.

Classical Splendour

Gulf of Hammemet, Hammemet, Tunisia

Interior designer Giorgio Pes renovated and decorated his Tunisian medina residence in pure Mediterranean white, mixing Arab and Roman elements and motifs, and turning its roof terrace into an outdoor living- and dining-room.

Restored and renovated, a Tunisian seaside villa maintains all the traditional characteristics of local Arab architecture while offering an immersion in the Classical world. Giorgio Pes, a Rome-based interior designer, has made a mix of ancient Roman and Arab motifs into a magical white-on-white eyrie overlooking the blue sea.

Narrow streets lead to the house, which is meshed in amongst other boxy white vernacular structures at land's edge between town and sea. Like the typical Arab house, the whitewashed residence appears closed from the outside, with small windows, few doors and antique wood and metal detailing painted the traditional powder-blue.

Tunisia has played host to a multitiude of cultural traditions. Hammamet, on the north-east coast, is a beach town with a medina, or old quarter, built within its ancient ramparts. Pes, who was able to obtain precise and accurate work from the talented local craftsmen, embellished the house with seductive Arab and Roman fragments. Statues, bronzes, terracottas and decorative motifs reveal the designer's predilection for the Neoclassical style.

The so-called *skita* inside the entrance door is a small room which separates the outdoors from the domestic interior. The Antique presence of Tunisia is felt in this tiny space. A fish in the ancient mosaic paving represents the seaside location and good luck.

From the *skita,* a Tunisian patterned wood door leads up stone stairs to the grand salon overlooking the sea. The room appears quite broad, with sheer glazed windows opening one entire side to the view. Only a grand Roman-arched fireplace, framing stone columns and swags of gathered white drapery impinge on the breadth of this vista. These design elements make the sea – as natural as it is – appear as if it is part of a grand theatre set. The sea is also visible from the dining-room. A pair of fluted Doric columns lead into this space, whose walls and rug are dominated by Tunisian geometric patterns.

The terrace becomes an outdoor living- and dining-room with white latticework overhead and at the sides. The white canvas draperies gathered in the corners can enclose the space like an Arab tent in bad weather or if the evenings are cool. However, in Hammamet's protected gulf, the harsh edges of the Mediterranean climate are much diminished.

Pes's reputation as an antiquarian and restorer sometimes obscures his background as a set designer for the cinema industry. But this aspect is clear at Hammamet, where he has glamorized a typical Arab house and captured a dramatic view of the sea.

above Pes's multi-cultural collections include an eighteenth-century Syrian chest inlaid with ivory, mother-of-pearl and silver displaying antique incised crystal bottles.

right 'It pleases me to present the antique with a greater sense of creativity, mixing styles and periods,' Pes says. A corner of the grand salon features a combination of Arab and classical European traditions: an English eighteenth-century Arab portrait, a nineteenth-century French gilded bronze clock and a small eighteenth-century writing chest inlaid with ivory, ebony and olive woods in Arab motifs.

opposite Expansive floor-to-ceiling glass walls open the grand salon to the sea, framed by Corinthian columns. Billowing draperies and white slipcovers on the large sofas Pes designed add to the luxurious setting. The Roman-style fireplace displays antique plates, and a Turkish glass-and-brass lamp decorates the ceiling.

above Fluted Doric columns, white curtains and marble floors provide a Classical framework for the dining-room.

left Local Tunisian decorative arts furnish the dining-room, including antique majolica wall tiles and gold-and-crystal dinner-ware.

opposite Marble and majolica tiles form the walls of the master bath. Working with local craftsmen for the entire renovation, Pes found that age-old Tunisian decorative traditions for precision and detail were still alive and well.

Of Coves and Caves

Santa Monica Bay, Malibu, California

Tan-grey concrete blends with the wet sand and rocky coves of Malibu, and the expansive roof of John Lautner's Beyer house mimicks the background Santa Monica Mountains as an expression of Lautner's unique principles of organic design.

The community of Malibu occupies a series of rocky points, shallow coves and sandy beaches facing south and west towards Santa Monica Bay and the Pacific Ocean along the Southern California coast. The pleasant climate makes surfing, spearfishing, diving, running and sunning possible year-round. The rural character of the hills nearby adds a primitive quality to the area, which was once inhabited by native Americans. Chumash names like Topanga, Zuma and Malibu itself still refer to the ancient trails which wind through canyons and down to private coves.

Residents Stanley and Lyn Beyer wisely listened to the advice of their interior designer, the late Michael Taylor, when he recommended the renowned California architect John Lautner as the perfect person to capture the true nature of their isolated ocean-front site. 'The site is thrilling,' Lyn Beyer says as she recalls their decision to ask Lautner to design their house. 'We feel like his design makes our house part of the landscape.' On its rocky point with patches of sandy beach and surf hitting the rocks in layers of white and blue, the house is indeed very contemporary without being hard-edge or high-tech in feeling.

Lautner's brand of modernism developed out of the organic principles of Frank Lloyd Wright, his teacher and one-time employer. A shaped concrete roof balances over glass walls and comes down to the ground at various points around the house's multiple sides. The rough tan-grey concrete blends with the colour of the wet sand. This expansive canopy mimicks the nearby Santa Monica Mountains. 'The design is a segment of a cylinder, tilted up and then cut to create an irregular perimeter,' the late architect explained. 'It appears both natural and timeless.' The curved roof line also acts as a protective cover over part of the ocean-front terrace, where a concrete table surrounded by cylindrical concrete stools is used for outdoor dining. Little maintenance is involved to keep the concrete surfaces and concrete-and-slate terraces in good order.

Inside, the living-room is like a spacious theatre focused on the continuous performance of the surf pounding at the rocky point. This view is especially enjoyable from a portion of the living-room that perches over Santa Monica Bay. The light changes continually in a delightful way. Together with Lautner, Taylor, who designed the interiors, imported large river boulders to the site and placed them throughout the house. The floors also have a natural appearance, being made of concrete and sawn slate polished to glisten like the ocean waves.

Lautner appreciated architecture without limits or superficial connections to fads or movements. He inherited the concept of the open plan and connection to nature from Wright. Yet while Wright always spoke and wrote about the earth, Lautner, in his siting of this house, orientated his architecture to the water. His fluid plan opens up the waterfront side to the view by means of glass and curved terraces with glass railings. The building both fits into the curves of the coves and balances out over the rocks and surf, its design echoing the organic character of the tidal waters.

above With the roof suspended above the continuous glass walls around much of the house, the interiors seem open to the Pacific. In the living-room, the curved banquette of a conversation area is perched out over the water and piled with large pillows.

right A protective concrete roof, continuous glass and textured concrete walls follow the coastline. Irregular rocks and the ever-changing surf form an organic foundation for the house.

opposite above A wide curved soffit creates a protective canopy above the bed in Lyn and Stanley Beyer's master bedroom. Skylights and glass walls fill the room with light, and a concrete fireplace warms the room on cool and rainy Californian days.

opposite In the spacious living-room space, the all-encompassing curving concrete roof balances over the glass walls. Large river boulders were placed throughout the interiors, and the floors are made of concrete and sawn slate. The furnishings represent the frequently copied 'California Style' of the late interior designer Michael Taylor. They include white canvas upholstery, overscaled sofas and chairs, peeled-log-and-rush chairs and plexiglass or free-form granite low tables.

Villa Kerylos

Port of Fourmis, Beaulieu-sur-Mer, France

In the first decade of the 1900s, archaeologist Theodore Reinach built an ancient Greek house on a French Mediterranean coast which reminded him of Corinth. Two roof terraces with pergolas permitted Reinach to admire the exceptional site.

On a rocky peninsula projecting into the Mediterranean, archaeologist Theodore Reinach built a caprice – a folly – at the beginning of this century. This waterside house exactly reconstructs a Greek house of the second century BC.

Reinach built the house at the foot of dramatic cliffs on a coast which, he said, reminded him of the coast of Corinth. He worked with architect Emmanuel Pontromoli, one of his colleagues at the Academy of Beaux-Arts in Paris, and was aided by various specialists in Classical studies and building crafts: fresco painting, stucco working, marble and bronze working and furniture making. Although Reinach wanted modern comforts as well, such as electricity, running water and a telephone service, the materials and features are otherwise true to period, except for the glass windows, which in Antiquity would have been of oiled papyrus.

During his regular vacations to the spot, Reinach dressed in Classical Greek style – as did his guests. Neither megalomaniac nor eccentric, he was from a wealthy, educated family, a member of the class of scholarly gentlemen like Jules Verne and Gustave Eiffel, all of them rich, knowledgeable and poetically inclined.

The plan of the house is based on one built in ancient times for a wealthy citizen of Delos. Around the atrium patio, the principal rooms – a library, dining-room and living-room – are distributed on the ground floor, and the bedrooms, baths and studies are found on the first floor. Next to the *triklinos*, or dining-room, is the living-room or grand salon, which, Vitruvius tells us, was reserved for use by men. The salon's interior is spectacular, with walls painted to simulate Tuscan marble and a mosaic representing Theseus slaying the Minotaur. The 'Classical' furniture – tables, seats, a bed and also a throne for the master bath – are made of exotic woods, bronze and ivory. An altar of Carrara marble is also located in the salon, and on each side of it, doors give access to the *oikos*, a very small, personal salon which opens to the garden by means of a large glazed door. From here, a beautiful view unfolds to the charming port of Fourmis.

The Mediterranean setting and view of the sea are key to the house's design. The garden, some of the windows and the terraces offer views of the coast from Cap Ferrat to Monaco. Also open to the vast marine horizon, the library windows are orientated to the east to permit working in the morning hours. The library occupies the height of a floor and a half with a gallery space. The most lofty view from the house is from the two roof terraces with pergolas.

Reinach died in 1928, and his house was classified as a historic monument in 1966, when it was left to the Institute of France, a group of five academies dedicated to letters and the arts and sciences. Since 1967, the house has been open to the public. The Villa Kerylos is the most remarkable reconstruction of an ancient Greek dwelling in modern times. No museum in Greece itself evokes the daily life of its ancient citizens so completely. The house represents an entirely accurate evocation of ancient furniture, mosaics and frescoes – all creating a striking image of a timeless seaside hideaway.

opposite Windows on one side of the grand salon look out to the Mediterranean and the port of Fourmis while the doors on the opposite wall open to the atrium. The interior appears to be an archaeologically correct interpretation of Greek domestic architecture. Its walls are painted to resemble Tuscan marbles with a meander-pattern cornice and the central floor mosaic border. Three Antique-style chandeliers hang from the decorative coffered ceiling, and *klismos* chairs, Classical tables and couches are made of exotic woods, bronze and ivory.

right A pair of Ionic columns flank the bed in one of the first-floor bedrooms. The mosaic floor creates a pattern of intertwined vines like the decoration of the ceiling beams. The murals depict early Greek motifs.

below Located at one end of the grand salon is a Carrara marble altar, left, which is raised on a marble platform. The glass-and-bronze door, right, offers a glimpse of the atrium.

below right Reinach wanted all the amenities of modern times, such as running water, and each large bathroom has a stone tub set on lion's feet, with dolphin spouts and swan's-head handles in silver.

A Medina Cottage

Atlantic Coast, Asilah, Morocco

Ramparts separating the old quarter of Asilah village from the Atlantic surf protect an exotic retreat for two French couples. It is merged with a neighbourhood of white cubic houses having tiny windows, blue trim and crenellated roof lines.

The jetty at Asilah projects like a finger out into the Atlantic. Located on the coast of Morocco approximately nineteen miles south of Tangiers, the village is composed of buildings set like white cubes on rocks behind a rampart. The town has a tumultuous past: it was first Portuguese, then Spanish, then Moorish. Recently, the Moroccan government has preserved the medina, or old quarter, restoring the houses to their original small scale and white-washed purity with green or blue trim and shutters.

One residence was restored by a couple and two talented friends, Françoise Dorget and Charles Chauliaguet. Françoise Dorget, owner of Caravane in Paris, a shop with textiles from all over the world, had become intrigued with Asilah's particular style and the northern Rif region many years earlier. She and her architect-husband, Charles Chauliaguet, studied the village's architecture in order to reproduce its elements for their friends' residence.

Chauliaguet found himself following local building traditions since the Moroccan masons could not read his plans. The town is humid during winter storms, breakers often protect the windows of the sea-front houses, and water runs down the inner face of the rampart. The masons built double-thick walls of breeze blocks, and the corrosive weather conditions forced them to use more expandable wood for door frames. Windows were designed in traditional style.

Only one door leads into the original two-storey house from the six-foot-wide passageway separating it from the rampart. The ground floor includes the living-room, which becomes a master bedroom during the winter when it is warmer there than on the upper storey. Of the ground-level patio, Dorget says, 'It is very calm, never windy and never too sunny. So the patio is quiet, and there we have lots of birds.'

To reach the upper bedrooms, an open-air staircase ascends to a small terrace like a sheltered landing with cotton awnings. It is open on the west side to the sea and on the east side to the patio. This terrace lies between green and blue bedrooms. A second staircase leads up to the roof terrace, which serves as a 'garden' as in typical Arab houses. There, like a cubic lookout tower above the terraces, an upper room serves as an office and occasional guest-room. 'The terraces overlooking the sea offer another atmosphere compared to the patio,' says Dorget. 'There is quite a strong wind with the hot sun and the sea. It always seems different.' She continues, 'It is very pleasant from March and April – and also October is nice – because the light is so beautiful during these months. Even if it is a little cold in the evenings, it is always very sunny during the day. And almost half of the year it is quite warm for swimming. One thing to remember is that Asilah is on the Atlantic Ocean. It is very much an ocean, and the weather is very strong ... Like Brittany, this area has the rocks, cliff and strong sea. It can be quite rough, like being out in the open ocean. Also when there is high tide or low tide, everything can change along the beach, all the time and each hour.'

opposite The rugged Atlantic coast is best appreciated from the first-storey terrace and a pair of roof terraces linked by a bridge designed by architect Charles Chauliaguet, who renovated the cottage and shares it with his wife, Françoise Dorget, and the French couple who own the house. The first-storey terrace, located between two bedrooms, is sheltered by the bridge and by cotton awnings and is furnished with a dining table and café chairs from the Rif region.

above A traditional Moroccan niche with animal sculptures decorates the small ground-floor living-room, or salon, where double doors open to the patio. 'All fabrics and furnishings are from Asilah, Tangiers or nearby towns in the Rif Valley,' says Françoise Dorget, owner of Caravane, a Paris shop with international textiles. Dorget designed the banquette and chose all the furnishings, such as the small tables and chest.

right 'We thought it nice to have everything made by the peasant craftspeople who live here,' says Dorget. A desk and chair in a corner of the blue bedroom display the contemporary local style.

above A model of a local fishing boat christened 'Rosa' is one of the few decorative items in the spare and airy green bedroom. Appearing like portholes with ocean views, the tiny windows are typical of the style of the old medina, as is the tiled basin, right.

right The tiled built-in basin of one bathroom has pierced cedar cabinet panels, and the floor is a patchwork of tile fragments.

above Perched above the roof terraces is an isolated cubic lookout tower. Used as a study and occasional guest-room, it has a beamed ceiling, brick floor and small wall niches, and is furnished with a Morroccan chest, Rif-region chairs and local fabrics for drapery and bed coverings. Doors and windows open the lone tower to the roof terraces and the ocean.

right *Zeliges*, or colourful Moroccan tiles, decorate the walls and basin of the first-floor bathroom for the blue bedroom. The storage cabinet is enclosed with traditional Moroccan pierced cedar door panels.

Sybaritic Suite
Caribbean Sea, Santo Domingo, Dominican Republic

Breezy pavilions and stone forts of the Spanish settlers inspired French architect Savin Couelle to design Nathan Moore's family retreat near Santo Domingo as tile-roofed pavilions with open sides facing terraces, pools and the ocean.

'always use the natural material of the country where I work,' says French architect Savin Couelle, who practises in Turin and along the Costa Smeralda of Sardinia. 'Since I adapt to the country where I work, in the Dominican Republic, I designed a Dominican house.'

The Caribbean beach house he designed near Santo Domingo is for three generations of the family of Mr and Mrs Nathan Moore. While the exteriors and plan reflect the order and regional features of the Dominican vernacular, the interiors convey the organic, sculptural quality for which the French architect is known.

'I design houses to correspond to the climate and at the same time to correspond with the client's desires and needs,' Couelle says. The Moores knew his houses on the Costa Smeralda and wanted a similar beach house, but Couelle felt that his design should respond to the local vernacular. 'As a Dominican house, it is set flat and continuous to the ground, and – like open pavilions – it is completely transparent, so that the wind flows through the house. Since there was a big green lawn to the sea and a group of houses nearby, I didn't want to marry the house primarily with the land or only with the village of houses,' the architect observes.

Couelle initially spent a week getting to know the island, seeing the formidable stone ruins of Spanish forts and learning the traditions of the Spanish settlers, who built breezy pavilions with the assistance of shipbuilders. With these traditions in mind, he decided to raise the ground level of the house in order to relate it to a nearby palm forest and the ocean.

An outer wall of coral with an iron gate forms the entrance to the front garden, and the door beyond is rendered in typical Spanish fashion of wrought-iron and glass. The entrance is part of a higher pavilion with a roof-top terrace. To one side of it is a wing containing the master bedroom suite and, to the other side, further bedrooms and servants' rooms.

On the ocean side of the house, terraces run along the three pavilion façades below tiled roofs, and a swimming pool and lap pool create a smooth transition to the Caribbean. Polished coral blocks set between the pools provide space for sunning.

The walls of the house are built of two layers of quarried coral, forming interior living areas with lofty ceilings and open archways. Arched openings to the terraces are enclosed by natural-stained louvred doors. Couelle detailed the interiors with brickwork and wooden doors patterned in the Spanish manner. Some ceilings are supported by beams of *pancho prieto,* a native hardwood logged decades ago for an unfinished railroad. The dining area features a beamed ceiling of a rare wood which was once exported to Spain for building caravels.

Ships are alluded to throughout the house, which Couelle has compared to a boat at anchor. The architect even created a child's room with a loft reached by a ship's ladder. While each bedroom has a patio for showering, sunning or eating, the master bedroom features broad arched openings to view the pools, the lawn, an adjoining golf-course and the ocean. 'I like to plant houses in the ground,' Couelle explains. 'My dream is to relate a house to the land and to the water view.'

left At night, over the reflections of the pool, the living-room and terrace glow with light. Coral piers, the lofty ceiling and open archways define the space, while tile floors, brickwork, patterned wooden doors and the wrought-iron-and-glass front door reflect Spanish influence.

right A glimpse through an arched portal shows the entrance garden between the house and the outer coral wall with its lush planting and subterranean character.

below The master bedroom suite makes up one of the pavilions and features broad arched openings to the terrace. When the louvred doors are open, the tile-floored bedroom has a clear view to the pools and the ocean.

Villa Rocca nel Circeo

Tyrrhenian Sea, Sabaudia, Italy

Monte Circeo and the Tyrrhenian Sea are the setting for Count Giovanni Volpi's home at the unspoiled village of Sabaudia. Built by his mother in 1955, the temple-like pavilion and side wings fulfilled her vision in a Palladian manner.

Count Giovanni Volpi recalls growing up on the Tyrrhenian seashore at Villa Rocca nel Circeo, the classical villa his mother, Countess Nathalie Volpi, built in 1955 with architect Tomaso Bruzzi to fulfill her vision of ancient architecture as interpreted by Palladio. 'It's a version of a Palladian design, a central colonnaded pavilion with side wings,' says Count Volpi, who now maintains the beach house as his own.

Nathalie Volpi had fallen in love with Sabaudia, a village located halfway between Rome and Naples. The village provides the charm of a tiny community only sixty miles south-east of Rome. Countess Volpi bought up as much land at Sabaudia as she could in the mid-1950s, thus creating a thirty-acre site which extends from the Tyrrhenian Sea to Lake Sabaudia.

The classical villa which the Countess constructed at the seashore also relates to the nearby lake by means of a tunnel. Count Volpi's childhood memories include picnics at the lake, where a pavilion commands a view of the ruins of a villa which belonged to the Roman general and epicure Lucullus.

Countess Volpi used to drive here from Rome in her cane-covered Fiat and fill the house with guests. Her son has preserved the tradition of Volpi hospitality and the dramatic simplicity of the structure and interiors.

Roman-style brickwork clads the tunnel which leads from the house on the dunes under the coast road to Lake Sabaudia's edge. The same brickwork flanks the walls of the ceremonial drive which leads to the villa's main entrance. Inside, Pompeiian-style furnishings predominate, with crimson hangings which confer an austere, regal character on the high-ceilinged classical spaces. There are Roman capitals and sculptures throughout the house, and the colour of the drapery fabric was borrowed from that of the cape linings of Roman Imperial cavalrymen.

The winter dining-room opens on to a terrace which is used for candlelit dining during the summer. Most rooms in the villa have sea views, especially the symmetrical grand salon. Here, travertine floors are set in a herringbone pattern, and the ceiling is groin-vaulted. A grand staircase leads from the salon to the upstairs guest-rooms, which are furnished with seventeenth-century pieces. Red draperies hang from bronze spikes and contrast with the white stucco walls and travertine floors. Expansive sea views from the window balustrades convey the impression of being aboard a ship.

The backdrop to the villa and the ocean view is Monte Circeo and the wild natural landscape. The villa itself is surrounded by dunes that cannot support lush gardens, and thus the architecture is seen in stark relationship to the landscape, where the changing light creates shifting patterns on the temple-like forms.

In this minimal setting, the striking colonnaded porch of the central block seems to hover like a mirage above the sandy beach. In one corner of the porch, chaise-longues covered in the Volpi family colours furnish the space, while campaign chairs surround a patinated bronze table with a stone capital as its base. The porch's Ionic columns frame views overlooking the seascape, and broad stairs lead nobly down to the sand and sea.

opposite The colonnaded porch of the central structure becomes the focus of life by the sea. One corner is furnished with collapsible campaign chairs surrounding a bronze tray table with a stone capital base. Architect Tomaso Bruzzi originally designed the house.

above The classical interiors are dramatic with 'Caraboniere'-red draperies hanging from bronze spikes and contrasting with the white walls and travertine floors. The side-table and chair in black leather are both in seventeenth-century style.

right A corner of the grand salon opens to the sun porch and the view through cross-mullioned windows. The banquettes with travertine bases rest on travertine floors set in a herringbone pattern. Capturing the ancient spirit, stools like Greco-Roman campaign chairs surround the bronze tray table.

An Organic Fantasy

Port la Galère, Cannes, France

Overgrown with vegetation, the earth-coloured forms merge with the rocks and curves of the Port La Galère coast where Hungarian-born architect Antti Lovag designed and built this classic example of organic modernism in 1970.

'When building by the sea, the curved forms of nature are the right forms for architecture,' says Antti Lovag of the summer house he designed and built in 1970 at Port la Galère on the Côte d'Azur near Cannes. The house, now a fine example of 1970s modernism, appears both organically grown and high-tech.

There are no façades in the traditional sense, since the house is composed of curved and spherical forms upon which one is able to climb and walk about with very little effort. Since the walls, roof, doors and windows are bubble-like in appearance, this well-grounded home has gained the reputation of being *extra*-terrestial.

Lovag, never a fan of standard formal conventions, was born in Hungary and studied in Sweden and France. His style matured during his years of collaboration with architect-ecologist Jacques Couelle, designing organically shaped houses which merge with their seaside locations.

Lovag rebels against pure geometry and believes that architectural forms should reflect the flexibility of nature, basing his conceptions on the curves of the human body. To this end, he employs the modern technology of reinforced concrete, which permits rich variations in shape. He is perfecting the use of a 'knit' synthetic technique which renders concrete supple and flexible in shape. To create these sorts of spaces, he employs hundreds of curved steel strips as an armature for his structures, building them like giant plaster sculptures. Between the exterior concrete surfaces and interior concrete and stucco, these metal skeletons provide ancillary spaces for utility services, such as gas and water pipes and electrical conduits.

Inside, this house is also composed of spherical forms, reached via cylindrical corridors and oval doors. It is unclear where walls end and ceilings and floors begin. Rooms were placed, measured and modified while construction was in progress; windows were planned to make the best use of light. 'Volumes were adjusted to the configuration of the site, and the house developed in a spontaneous manner,' explains Lovag. 'The entire structure represents a natural evolution.'

Maintaining the sculptural effect, most of the furniture is built in with curved banquettes and circular tables. 'Traditional furniture of the rectilinear type is without use here,' Lovag observes. Living, dining and kitchen spaces are on the ground floor, and a stair – reminiscent of the ribbed configurations of a snail's shell – leads from these spaces to four bedrooms above. The marine horizon is visible through large oval and round doors and windows which evoke the appearance of portholes.

Vegetation grows over the earth-coloured masses of the house, and irregular pavers of travertine form paths which mediate between it and its seaside setting. Lovag did not wish to deform the site with traditonal platform foundations, preferring to utilize the rocks as an essential element of the construction. So the house and outdoor pool follow the curves of the terrain. 'Natural erosion creates a world of curves,' says Lovag. 'The house and the paths, situated in a slight hollow of a hill, seem like the furrows of the nearby cliffs. And like the cliffs and the sea, the house appears as if it has been here for centuries.'

opposite top Antti Lovag feels that curved natural forms are most appropriate for architecture when building by the sea. The entrance hall includes a form for the stairway to the four upstairs bedrooms, and its protected shell and ribbed interior shape evoke the configurations of a nautilus shell.

opposite Circular doors and cylindrical corridors connect the spaces of the ground-floor living-rooms. The den features layers of sculptural built-in, curved banquettes and circular tables. An upper shelf holds a curved 'hammock' which has its own window to the sea view.

above The conversation area of the main salon is a circle of banquettes with a large window facing the sea. The organic character of the room makes it unclear where walls end and ceilings begin. 'Reinforced concrete permits rich variations in shape, like the curves of the human body,' says Lovag.

opposite A viewing banquette faces an elliptical window looking over the trees to the sea. 'Windows were planned according to the best orientation to the view and the light and developed spontaneously as the house was built,' Lovag explains. 'The entire structure represents a natural evolution.'

left One bathroom is entered through an elliptical door. Lovag constructed the curved and cylindrical spaces by creating armatures for the shapes with hundreds of curved steel strips, like a giant plaster sculpture.

below The bathroom gives the impression of a seamless, continuous construction, much like that on boats. A small porthole-type window adds to the nautical effect.

IF House

Indian Ocean, Talpe, Sri Lanka

A verandah house located on the sandy beaches of the village of Talpe enjoys a garden paradise of coconut palms, remnants of the plantation culture introduced to the southern region of Sri Lanka when it was a British colony.

The name "IF" comes from this magnificent [Rudyard] Kipling poem about maintaining oneself with "head held up high" through life's challenges,' says David Gerard, one of the owners of this house in Talpe, a village in the forested, humid southern portion of Sri Lanka. The entire island is fringed by lagoons, sand-bars, peninsulas, dunes and marshes; forests and grasslands cover seventy per cent of it.

'The history of this house,' Gerard continues, 'is that it was built about ten years ago by a Norwegian film producer and a Norwegian film star. And the house looks like a much older structure because they went around Sri Lanka, studied all of the architecture and designed the house to incorporate regional colonial elements. Since we bought the house about five years ago, we have designed and added a pavilion where we eat which is in the grass area away from the house, and the old kitchen was turned into a bedroom. We put in a lovely new kitchen, which is separate altogether, behind the dining pavilion. All of our additions were done in the same style of the existing house.'

The original pavilion-style house has a tiled roof over a high-ceilinged structure with covered porches all around. Since the region is humid and warm throughout the year, each room has – instead of windows – air circulation from the porches through wide, segmental-arched openings which are infilled with wooden shutters.

The angled grid of large stone pavers further unites the spatial flow of the interior rooms out to the exterior porches, while the chocolate-brown colour of the tiles above is matched by the pavers' deep earthen colour – all of which unites the house with the rich colours of the surrounding forest.

Two of the house's other three owners, Barbie Gall and Anne Gerard, undertook the design of the interior themselves, reworking the main pavilion with some of the furniture purchased by the original owners. The porches are furnished with chaises in the traditional Sri Lankan form: low, with angled backs and elegantly curved arms. 'It's all quite casual,' says Anne Gerard about the decor, 'and those wonderful chairs are very standard for the region. Ours are antique, and you cannot find these pieces outside the country.'

Settled by Sinhalese, Tamils and Europeans, Sri Lanka has experienced political unrest in recent years. 'The problems are up north around the Jaffna Peninsula,' David Gerard explains, 'and so when we visit our home, it's just a lovely, peaceful place, and we don't know that anything is going on up north.' The monsoons from May to October don't bother the Gerards and Galls, who find that December and March are their two favourite months to visit. 'We like to come here at Christmas and Easter,' says David Gerard. 'At the holidays, we have a wonderful time getting together on these sandy shores of the Indian Ocean.'

above The Indian Ocean is the focus of the house's sprawling stone-paved terrace where stairs, right, lead to the beach. The outdoor living spaces include stone couches and a tile-roofed pavilion. The circular fountain is framed by palms whose fronds create a virtual ceiling over this outdoor 'room'.

left Washed by the sea and shaded by palms, this haven inspires artists and adventurers just as ancient Ceylon appealed to seekers of the lost paradise like Marco Polo.

opposite top Adapting a regional plan, tile-paved verandahs surround all sides of the house, forming a high-ceilinged living-room with regularly spaced arched openings for air circulation and views of the forest and the ocean. The white-washed room is furnished with four large couches. At the centre, two solid wood triangles are set together to form a low, square table.

opposite The verandah is a wrap-around, open-air living-room formed by tall, slender columns, sheer draperies and adjustable grass shades. Antique plantation chaises look out to the ocean and the dense vegetation.

Views from the Terrace

As virtual outdoor rooms, waterside terraces, porches and balconies provide wondrous places to read, eat, sun or enjoy cocktails and conversation. Most especially, they provide magical vantage points from which to enjoy views of the water. Stone balustrades, turned-wood balusters, metal railings and plexiglass panelling are amongst the traditional and modern elements which define the character of terraces and balconies. The occasional canvas awning, swagged covering or umbrella provides temporary protection from changing light or climate conditions.

The word 'terrace' evokes a narrow level of earth usually overlooking a steep embankment down to a river, lake or sea. Manmade terraces, along with smaller porches and balconies, attached to houses located by the water provide a physical and visual link between it and the land. They are literally extensions out into watery space. These building forms can transform a residence from a self-contained, protective environment into a dynamic and dramatic setting for enjoying the ever-changing interrelationship amongst water, earth and air.

Safe Havens

I rregular coastlines with marginal seas, shielded bays and river mouths provide excellent natural harbours. Since these bodies of water are connected with the oceans by means of straits or other openings, navigation through them has played an important part in dispersing cultures around the world. Gulfs and their port cities have contributed to the history and development of civilization, especially in the lands bordering the Mediterranean Sea and the coastal regions of India, China and Japan.

Any concavity of a coastline may be called a gulf or, if small, a bay. Natural harbours like New York Bay, as it was christened by the explorer Giovanni da Verrazano, provide calm waters for sheltering ships. Today, engineers can also create artifical harbours with still waters at economical locations by building solid or floating breakwaters and jetties. Whether by gradual or sudden transition from water to land, gulfs and bays provide inhabitants of and visitors to harbour cities with various approaches, whether docks or piers, jetties or moored ships.

Harbours have developed into two basic types. The first provides transportation of cargo and passengers, fishing opportunities and marinas for mooring ships, while the second protects the land from sea encroachment or maintains river estuaries. Since shrimp, oyster and other fisheries are concentrated in many gulfs where nutrients gather and fish feed in quantity, wharves, boardwalks and piers provide places from which to fish as well as allowing pedestrians to walk near the water's edge and give ports or harbours distinct personalities.

Protected harbours and ports with extensive residential developments are found around the world. Hong Kong, especially, has an unusually intimate connection with the water. The scale of its buildings ranges from financial towers and high-rise apartment blocks to industrial structures and a port crowded with freighters, steamers and tankers juxtaposed with smaller junks and recreational yachts. All of these contrast with the natural mountain-side setting of Victoria Peak and the bay. Surprisingly, modern Hong Kong can be compared with the quaint fishing village of Portofino because, despite the contrast of size, the two places have inseparable relationships with their respective harbours. Portofino is built around a small bay on the Ligurian coast of Italy. The town faces its sheltered cove with virtually no separation from it. Between town and water is a narrow pavement, laid out in a gentle arc which leads to the central piazza. Narrow streets wind up the hill and blocks of houses rise up in a collage of tinted stucco.

The unique single-family houses built in private harbours along gulfs or bays near such cities as Hong Kong or Portifino share the colourful traditions of each area. Regional attitudes towards interrelationships with or separation from the water are as important as the forms and materials of such houses in defining their identity.

Red Oaks

Little Harbour, Cohasset, Massachusetts

A granite outcropping at the edge of a Massachusetts harbour forms the foundation of a 1906 house recently renovated by Robert A. M. Stern. Its Shingle Style massing with Georgian details features a broad, white, wood-trimmed terrace on the harbour.

'Cohasset is a beautiful town, originally a resort and now a suburb. It was one of the defining coastal places where in the late nineteenth century Americans came to terms with their colonial past,' explains Robert A. M. Stern, who renovated a house in this New England harbour town between 1992 and 1996. 'This house was originally built in 1906 for a Boston family who summered at Cohasset,' Stern continues. 'An earlier ballroom was, with regret, taken down, but it blocked views and darkened the interiors.' Its removal opened up the view for the new living-room with a deep side porch with Tuscan columns. In place of the ballroom is a new formal garden and pool with a west-facing harbour view. Stone outcroppings and pavers outlined with grass surround the pool.

The house's interiors reflect the style of Ogden Codman, the great turn-of-the-century American decorator. A small existing study was panelled in cherry, and each fireplace was given an intricately carved mantel. The master bedroom received a vaulted ceiling and a bay window to expand the view. Carved dolphins and boats decorate the hall panelling. 'The entrance hall is one of the best rooms of the original house,' says Stern, 'and some of that woodwork is old and some is new. You can't quite tell what is new or old. It all looks as if it is a grand old house which has just been freshened up by new owners. In fact, that's just the effect we had in mind.' Stern worked with Randy Correll, project architect.

The house is Shingle Style with Georgian details. The grey shingle cladding is offset by a tall stone chimney and white wooden window and door trim surrounding the many generous openings – including several oculi – which provide a multitude of framed views of the water. The massing of the house is assymetrical, with bay windows and dormers, a widow's walk, an added conservatory, a broad terrace facing the harbour view to the south and a number of low, gabled roof lines. Surrounding the house are gardens with stone and wood rail fences.

Red Oaks invites comparison with historic Beauport, built in 1907 at Gloucester, Massachusetts, by Henry Davis Sleeper. 'A man like Mr Sleeper would think nothing of weaving together new and old, and new elements which looked old,' explains Stern. 'He pillaged other houses or bought parts of them, rescuing them from demolition. So this is an old New England tradition we followed at Red Oaks, and it makes it a palimsest, a layering of elements.' Like Beauport, Red Oaks has a spectacular site. 'The site is very special in the sense that it is wonderful to be up on that rock,' says Stern, describing the house's incomparable perch on a forty-foot-high granite outcropping.

opposite From the well-proportioned formal dining-room, double doors lead to the terrace and Little Harbor, around which the New England town of Cohasset grew up.

right Stern considers the entrance hall the best room in the original house, with successful hall panelling decorated with dolphins and boats carved in relief. The new elements are indistinguishable from the old, giving the additions integrity and the feeling of age.

below In the master bedroom, where the ceiling has recently been vaulted and a bay window added to expand the view, the furnishings and the renovations reflect the style of Ogden Codman, the renowned turn-of-the-century decorator.

Mediterranean White

Blau Sound, Menorca, Spain

One wing of an Iberian port house juts out on the water side where Oscar Tusquets and Carlos Diaz designed its corner patio to be closed off as necessary, since northern Menorca can be cold and windy in the winter. The furniture and silver service are also by Tusquets.

A tiny private dock links Casa Tula by means of a small staircase to the sea. 'Here, the house is high on a bluff, and its relationship is very close to the water,' says Barcelona architect Oscar Tusquets, who designed the Menorca Island house with his partner, Carlos Diaz. 'The location is Blau Sound, a natural port where the water is calm.' The house is likely to be the last on this Balearic island to be sited so close to the water. 'A new rigid law has forbidden the construction of anything within about 160 feet of the coast,' Tusquets adds.

The lucky owner of the house is an attorney who initially asked the late James Stirling to design a house for this site. When Stirling didn't have the time to do it, he suggested Tusquets. 'He came with a letter from James Stirling and I thought, "Someone who wanted a James Stirling design is likely an interesting client," so I took the project,' says Tusquets.

All of the living spaces of the house look out to sea, an arrangement which was intended from the very beginning. Tusquets and Diaz planned the building as a set of connected gabled structures, with one embracing gable connecting two gabled wings. On the land side, these two wings project from the central structure quite symmetrically, while on the port side, one wing juts out where the land falls away, while the other recedes to form a sun terrace. There is a clear geometry to the cubic gabled structures, and they all fit within the rectangular imprint of the foundation. 'I like both the view from the house to the sea and the view from the sea to the house,' says Tusquets.

One of the challenges facing the architects was how to deal with the weather, and the design and organization of the wings reflect their solution. 'Everyone thinks that the Balearic Islands have very good weather and climate, but this is not so in northern Menorca,' Tusquet explains. 'The weather is not year-round. It is quite cold with the north winds in the winter, while in the summer it is fantastic. To handle the two conditions of summer and winter, the main rooms are sited towards the sun and they have terraces, which are important for breezes in the summer when the sun is very strong and hot. The rooms can open up for air circulation. However, in the winter when the north wind is strong, the large terrace is protected by the other wing of the house. The dining-room is in the wing which is set back, so it is protected and warm but yet it has an open view.' Shutters close all of the expansive window walls during the winter and when the owner is away. The climate and weather also dictated the wind-, weather- and seawater-resistant garden. By utilizing indigenous plants, the landscaping was made to seem native to the area.

Transplanted to Menorca, however, is the eighteenth-century British classicism which inspired Tusquets and Diaz's design. The pedimented imagery came with British colonization. 'Although it is now a traditonal style of the island, it is not folk architecture and is not completely popular. However, I like this quite naïve neoclassical architecture,' says Tusquets. Relief sculptures by Juan Bordes in the pediment reflect the same naïveté. Mythical symbols for the wind and sun, they battle with the natural forces on this rugged Menorcan site.

opposite above left Seen at a distance above the popular natural port near Mahon – and with all its blue shutters closed – the geometry of two gabled parts of Casa Tula becomes apparent. Where one wing recedes, it forms a sun terrace. 'The main rooms are sited towards the sun, and they have terraces which are important for breezes in the summer,' says Tusquets. The pedimented style of the house is based on a Neoclassical design which was transplanted to the island when it was a British colony.

opposite above right Spaced wooden planks from an upper deck create delightful light patterns on a protected deck below. The resident furnished the house throughout with contemporary furniture and rugs by Tusquets and his contemporaries, including this 'Luna' rug and 'Solaria' chair and table.

opposite below left The grey marble tub and console of the master bath face out to the wooden sun-deck and views of Blau Sound. The metal plant sculpture is by Guillem Bonet and Alicia Nuñez.

opposite below right Continuous with the master bath, the bedroom includes a working area with a chair by Jorge Pensi and a sycamore writing secretary by Jaume Tresserra on the glass table. A framed view of the port is visible through the glass interior wall of the small verandah.

right Transparency is one theme which governs the design of walls and windows throughout the house, and in the kitchen a glass cabinet is located in the window over the sink, maintaining a water view. The 'Victoria' porcelain and crystal are by Tusquets.

An Architectural Line-Up

Sag Pond, the Hamptons, Sagaponack, New York

Fresh water from Water Mill and salt-water from the Atlantic meet in Sag Pond at Sagaponack, where Richard and Eileen Ekstract's house is a modern architectural compound of separate rooms designed by Agrest and Gandelsonas.

'This is probably the best water-front property that we've ever experienced,' says Richard Ekstract, a patron who knows well what he's talking about. 'We used to have a house on the ocean,' he continues. 'But looking out on the ocean during the winter can be bleak. Except for an occasional fishing trawler, there is not much to see out there. But on this pond, there's a constant changing of wildlife through all of the seasons.'

When Ekstract and his wife, Eileen, asked the team of Diana Agrest and Mario Gandelsonas to design a traditional house for their Sag Pond site, they were surprised by the final outcome – a house of many traditional parts, but dissected in an imaginative fashion. Despite its unexpectedness, the house was planned to take advantage of the inland site about a hundred feet from Sag Pond. 'We have seventeen pairs of French doors that go across the entire downstairs, so every room has a pond view except for one bedroom,' explains Richard Ekstract.

Agrest and Gandelsonas planned the rooms along the sides of a large, single-space building with wooden barrel vaulting which faces a swimming pool and acts as a central focus in a compound. Extending from it are a collection of separate rooms: a couple of wooden towers, one cylindrical glass tower containing a study, and a wooden room perched at the end of a land-locked pier overlooking the pond. A short distance from the house, a long wall recalling the buildings of Luis Barragán runs along the swimming pool next to a pair of wooden shacks – the cabana.

'There is a gazebo off the main bedroom, and we can easily walk outside and view nature. From many of the viewing spots, we can see the sunsets, which are quite beautiful. And there is also a home office upstairs which has a widow's walk which goes 360 degrees around, so there are some interesting pond views from those heights,' observes Richard Ekstract. 'We can see the distant ocean from the upstairs as well,' adds his wife. Since the water levels at the pond site are high, the Ekstract house has a reinforced basement, and, in case of storms, it is solidly constructed with steel and equipped to withstand 130-mile-per-hour winds.

Today, houses built on the pond have to be at least three hundred feet back, but the Ekstract house was grandfathered in by a previous house begun on the site twenty-five or thirty years earlier, so it is much closer to the pond than others in the area. 'We can see the currents change in the pond,' says Eileen Ekstract of the tidal impact of the ocean on it. 'This is a brackish pond,' her husband continues, 'which is fed on one end by water running down from the hill of Water Mill. And it is fed on the other end by the ocean, so the two waters meet. Here you can find pike, crab, clams and sea life like that. Mostly the fish they catch here is pike.' 'There is a tremendous amount of wildlife at this site,' adds Eileen Ekstract. 'We canoe and we do a lot of bird-watching because the pond attracts geese, swans, ducks and other birds,' says her husband. 'We have only one problem. Sometimes the migrating geese fly over early in the morning when we're still sleeping, and we hear this loud "Honk, honk, honk."'

left French doors create the side walls of the wooden barrel-vaulted living structure, which acts as the spine of the building compound. A large fireplace divides the structure, which is furnished with casual classics.

top At one end of the open living structure are the dining and kitchen areas, separated merely by kitchen counters. 'From here we can see plenty of wildlife,' says Eileen Ekstract, 'since geese, swans, ducks and other birds are attracted to the pond.'

above A land-locked pier leads from a lookout to the master bedroom with a study above surrounded by a widow's walk.

Torre Clementina

Côte d'Azur, Cap Martin, France

Reorientated to the sea with added pools and a subterranean grotto, Torre Clementina, a Romanesque villa at Domain de Cap Martin, has been renovated by Charles T. Young with David Martin and John Bolt.

'In the renovation, we reorientated Torre Clementina to the sea,' explains architect David Martin. Originally, the fanciful villa, designed by Lucien Hesse in the 1890s, had been orientated to the narrow entrance road, with a Gothic ruin forming a gated entrance. Over the last few years, the château-like structure has been renovated for an international client by Martin and Manhattan architect Charles T. Young. Young has remodelled it, adding follies, cloistered walkways, terraces, fountains, grottoes and landscaping to the original Romanesque elements. Excellent outlooks, terraces and pools connect the villa to a glamorous view of Monte Carlo and the sparkling Mediterranean.

Young and Martin worked with the picturesque building traditions, rubble masonry and quaint detailing inherent to the old villa. 'What is curious about this house is its *fin-de-siècle* romanticism and especially the fascination with the idea of ruins,' says Young, referring to the Gothic entrance and the castellated appearance of the original design, as well as to the grottoes and Roman viaducts found in the original gardens. 'We decided to add to the collection of follies ... Particularly in the gardens, we extended the form of these follies to include little towers, arches or gateways built to look like ruins.' The architects also reshaped the top of the building, taking away an added floor to make the volumes read more clearly. Wanting to add more rooms but in a way that did not change the house's character, they ingeniously scooped out a new floor underneath it by developing a plan that missed all the important existing foundations. They then created a huge terrace

and swimming-pool addition with a grotto on the side of the house facing the Mediterranean. 'In keeping with older, more enclosed traditional-style houses, this villa has an alternation of the sense of enclosure with the sense of vista,' says Young. 'It's much like a good stage set,' he continues. 'The view out of a window is framed like a picture.' When the architects reshaped the upper part of the house, they created lookout-like eyries on the upper floor and a terrace above the living-room so it would be possible to enjoy the distant views.

The relationship of the terraced gardens to the water was a given, but the architects enhanced their unique siting. 'It is rather amazing how the original landscape architect, Raffaele Maïnella, took a raw cliff face approximately 150 feet high and created a garden by first building these mansonry-arch viaducts and essentially creating a site for a garden where none had existed,' Young explains. He and Martin worked with landscape architect Robert Truskowski to revive the cliffside garden standing on masonry-arch viaducts – the ancient Roman method of building – with landscaping over the top surfaces to create a stepped garden with a zigzag path. On the descent, one discovers the arches in some cases made into grottoes. 'There is a sense of enclosure in the gardens where the mature planting has taken on room-like qualities, but then you come to a parting of the trees and you have this beautiful vista to the Mediterranean and to Monte Carlo,' says Young. 'So, in the development of the new parts of the project, we tried to retain and extend that alternation of enclosure and vista we found there and in the house itself.'

above The classical covered pool which extends out into the landscape of the lower level of the house was inspired by the grottoes and Roman viaducts found in the original gardens. Young co-ordinated the landscape for the interior – exterior follies and belvederes such as this one with landscape architect Robert Truskowski.

opposite The addition of the reflective terrace pool – as well as the subterranean pool, grotto, belvederes and terraces – make a special connection to the glamorous view and twinkling lights of Monte Carlo and the shimmering Mediterranean.

right The original château-like structure has Romanesque fortress towers and rubble masonry. 'The house's *fin-de-siècle* fascination with the idea of ruins inspired our additional follies, like the cloister walkway in the garden,' says Young.

left The final design is rich with the addition of the pool terraces, split stair, Roman arches and mosaic-tiled pools. The architects reshaped the top of the house, removing an upper floor added in the 1920s, and they dug out a new floor under the house which opens out to the grotto and swimming pool.

opposite From the added subterranean floor, the water vista continues from the Roman-style grotto with its rich mosaics to the pool and the Mediterranean.

Shingle-Style Update
Naragansett Bay, Newport, Rhode Island

Historic Newport is associated with the late-nineteenth-century Shingle Style, which developed there and around Boston. The style's towers, verandahs, window bays, and especially its gambrel roofs have been given a new interpretation by architect James Estes.

'Before we even cleared the land, Jim Estes climbed up on a maple tree so he could look out over the site and select the best way to direct the house,' says one of the residents of this Newport, Rhode Island, house set on the edge of Naragansett Bay. The house looks towards the south-west, to the open ocean and Block Island. It is on a long, thin lot which slopes westward towards a short ledge down to the shore. 'We moved here for the sunsets,' the resident continues. 'We're aware of the sky changing incrementally, and the better sunsets have clouds, even rain-clouds.' The owners wanted the vernacular Shingle Style, but they also wanted to push that style's formal boundaries.

The Shingle Style, which developed around Newport and Boston, Massachusetts, is characterized by the use of shingles as an all-over wall covering, the continuity of the exterior surface, and an open plan around an entrance hall. In addition to the gambrel roof, other aspects of Estes' design fit the Shingle-Style formula. As he describes it, 'Overriding the whole house are the two simple forms of the tower and gambrel, and joining it all together is the plastic, red cedar-shingle skin. The trim is minimal and the windows recessed in some areas to emphasize the shingles and the idea of their wrapping form.'

The entrance is carved out of the front, defining the curved stair, and on the water side, bays and porches are carved out, sometimes with angles and sometimes with curves, and the tower blends in to the main form. The kitchen, dining and family room merge as one large area, while the living-room is an informal common room. 'Our favourite room is in the south-west corner on the first floor,' says the resident. 'It's sunny and has the best view ... We have such a big view of the sky. It's wonderful to sit in the master bedroom and have windows almost 180 degrees around to watch thunderstorms come down the bay. The winds will be howling, but there is a security because we have very little exposure to the north, where storms usually come from.'

Natural planting around the house was done intentionally. During the summer, the terrace becomes an outdoor living-room from which to enjoy the view and landscape. 'We'll entertain there, and my husband routinely sits out and reads the paper in the morning during good weather,' says one of the residents. 'One of our favourite spring activities is watching the sailboats come back after the winter,' she continues. Newport is on a popular bay with plenty of boat life, and the International Americas Cup-class boats are towed out to sea for their trials right in front of the house.

'We also see the lobster fishermen with their pots,' says the resident, 'and in the fall, the loons come in from the lake regions. We watch them, and a variety of ducks and other birds, like red-breasted mergansers, king eiders, the common golden-eye duck and piping plovers. We also have harbour seals which settle on the rocks in the winter just down the cove.' This year-round house proves that living on the water provides a great way to start the day. 'My husband walks our dog on the beach most mornings,' says the resident. 'He puts on boots over his suit trousers and takes off for the beach.'

above The living-room creates a bay form which shapes an outdoor terrace. The bay is made up of traditional Shingle Style windows with multi-paned transoms. Casually orientated towards a stone fireplace, the room is an informal common space which merges with the kitchen, dining- and family-room on the other side of a common stair hall.

right An upper terrace with curved walls appears to be carved out of the structure. Connected to the master bedroom suite in the tower, it is one of the owners' favourite outdoor spaces from which to view the bay.

opposite top The large bay of the dining-room is located in the lower part of the tower. From here, the house looks towards the south-west, to the open ocean and Block Island. 'Typical of the Shingle Style, the interior trim emphasizes the various room forms,' explains the architect.

opposite 'From the bed, you have almost 180-degree views of the bay,' says one of the residents of the house of the deep bay windows of the master bedroom located in the tower.

Casa Blava

Costa Brava, Cape Creus, Cadaques, Spain

Casa Blava combines an Old-World spirit with town-house sophistication. Its defining elements are the tiles which pave its boathouse terrace and interiors and decorate its wainscots and doorways, and its ironwork painted powder blue.

Blava, the port area of Cadaques in Spain, is one of the best preserved and most typical fishing villages along the northern coast of the Mediterranean near the French border. Bougainvillaea and oleander are interspersed amongst the port's steep, narrow streets, which rise up from the waterside. White houses and apartments are available to rent, since the town offers no large hotels. On the corners and along the promenades, there are cafés and bars which are called 'cellars' since they were the local wineries until the nineteenth century.

Cadaques lies on the peninsula of Cape Creus, on a slope looking out to a bay, part of a rugged stretch of coast interspersed with coves called the Costa Brava. The area is rich in fish and shellfish with warm, humid weather nearly year-round. Its landscape includes shades of silvery green from the olive trees and the silvery blue from the endless horizon of the sea. Inland are forests, meadows and villages surrounded by agricultural lands, whilst seaside settlements remain small and quaint.

Casa Blava at the Catalan port has an Art Nouveau appearance. Geometric blue tilework distinguishes the house's windows and terrace railings, which are painted powder blue to match the tiles. The four-storey façade is quite symmetrical, but two wings vary in the shapes of their steep roofs and small attic windows. Placed between these windows are unique metal braces which extend from the roof beams to corbels. The house's roofs and corbeled eaves reflect medieval influence.

On the piano nobile, the central entrance door is crowned by exquisitely patterned blue-and-cream tiles, and stairs lead over a ground-floor passageway and down a short flight to the main terrace. Defined by an ornate metal-and-tile railing, the terrace is actually located on the roof of Casa Blava's boathouse with angled doors and windows only feet away from the water.

The interiors of the high-ceilinged piano nobile also appear to date from an earlier era. Gleaming wooden floors and the resident's nineteenth-century-style furnishings maintain the sense of Old-World charm.

Cadaques has Greek and Roman archaeological sites, and the ideals of ancient Rome were assimilated into Catalan culture, thus helping the country to survive the barbarian invasions which followed the Empire's collapse. Following the period of Muslim domination, Spain continued to develop a unique culture incorporating elements of both Islamic and classical civilization. In modern times, Cadaques was appreciated for its nonconformity and was 'discovered' by painters, artists and intellectuals who chose it for their residences. Salvador Dalí was born nearby at Figueres and spent much of his time at this fishing village when Cadaques became a centre for the avant-garde.

Local museums and galleries still embrace that reputation and count among Cadaques's famous past visitors the artists Picasso, Max Ernst, Marcel Duchamp, René Magritte and David Hockney, as well as composer John Cage. Albert Einstein also vacationed here and would use his free time to play his violin. Today, the Museum of Graphic Arts and the Arts Museum show works of local artists, and each August the port features an international music festival.

opposite A player piano, in the tiled music room at the end of the enfilade of the piano nobile, is provided with many musical choices stored in the cabinet beside it.

opposite below left The main salon of the high-ceilinged piano nobile is detailed with decorative tile wainscots and floors and ceilings with robustly detailed cornices.

opposite below right The large master bath has the original Old-World fixtures: a freestanding tub and pedestal sink. Tiles cover the floor, wall and cornice, and the high window looks out to the bay view.

right Owned by Agosto Marucci, the blue-and-white-tiled Casa Blava overlooking the busy Catalan port has a turn-of-the-century appearance except for the steep roofs and corbelled eaves, which reflect a lingering medieval influence. Tilework accents the house's windows, and terrace railings are powder blue. Stairs lead over a ground-floor passageway and down a short flight to the main terrace located above the boathouse.

A House for All Seasons

Puget Sound, Seattle, Washington

On a steep site with views of Puget Sound and the Olympic Mountains, Dr and Mrs Gilbert Roth's steel-and-glass house – designed by James Olson and Tom Kundig of Olson Sundberg Architects – is a three-level structure with wedge-shaped decks.

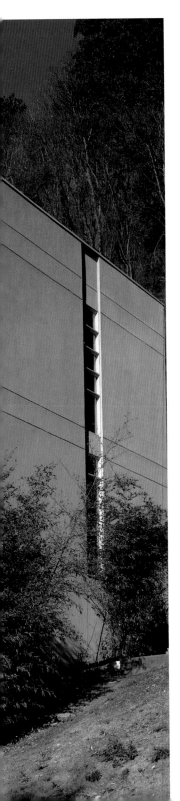

't's like living on an island unto itself,' explains Gilbert Roth of the house which he and his wife, Miriam, share near Seattle, Washington, on a narrow site which drops steeply to the west-facing beach front and looks out to spectacular views. 'I can honestly say the water never looks the same from one day to the next,' adds Miriam Roth. 'From the decks we can watch the ferries and shipping go by and in the winter view the snow-covered Olympic Mountains,' adds Gilbert Roth.

The contemplative, clean-lined architecture in metal and glass is the work of James Olson and Tom Kundig of the Seattle firm of Olson Sundberg Architects, with interiors by Terry Hunziker. 'Jim immediately expressed a vision of how the house ought to sit on the lot when he first visited the site,' says Gilbert Roth. 'Now when you come to the house from the street side, you come through a narrow, tall doorway and all of a sudden there's this spectacular view of the Sound.' He adds, 'We travel through the south of France and the Riviera and we wanted double French doors to a deck open to the water like those on the Riviera.' The Roths enjoy dining on the deck and are afforded privacy by the thick stucco exterior walls which extend from the house.

Olson and Kundig designed the house as a series of platforms above the site, extending into the natural environment on the decks which project from each level overlooking the gardens. 'I have a perennial garden up and down the hill since we have a sheltered climate,' says Miriam Roth. 'Because the weather will be warmer here by the water, we have a wonderful ability to have a yard full of flowers while we can have snow just up the hill.'

She adds, 'One of the things our guests find so fascinating when they walk out on to the decks is they feel like they are on a boat.' The metal railings as well as the lines of the windows appear ship-like on the south-west corner and west façade, which are opened up with glass.

On the interior, the south-west and west sides 'explode' with views, sunlight and the sounds of the surf through the carefully detailed and proportioned window walls. The best view of the water is through the double-height gallery wall, which provides one with a dramatic sense of being perched over the water, especially from the curved balcony of the master bedroom. No matter what level you are on, French doors open to a deck with a view. Each level has its own character; every room has lots of windows and a view of the Sound. The house is never dull or dark, and even during the winter, there is lovely light off the Sound, which has a silvery appearance at that time of year. During the colder months, the couple spend more time upstairs in the master bedroom suite enjoying the warmth of its fireplace and views of the mountains and Sound. During the summers, the middle-level living areas are filled with family and friends, as well as bright light and cool breezes.

The drama of the views, the seamlessness between the interior and exterior spaces, and the serendipitous light are what make this house so special. 'We can see when the rains are coming in and the wind blows up the water and gets wild and lashes up against the bulkhead,' says Miriam Roth. 'We see the sunsets and we see the weather in the making, and that's very exciting.'

above A catwalk bridge from the stairwell leads into the master bedroom suite, which takes up the entire upper level and includes a fireplace and a deck. Designer Terry Hunziker chose a subtle waterfall pattern for the carpet and the bedspread of the four-poster bed.

left Light filters into the living-room from the glass walls, and the metal railing of the terrace deck lends a ship-like feeling to the room.

opposite On entering the house through a 'pinched' entrance porch, a narrow, tall doorway opens to a spectacular view of the Sound, giving the sense of being perched over the water through a carefully proportioned nineteen-foot-high window wall. The curved master bedroom balcony enjoys the special view.

Framing the View

Determining how best to frame views of the water from a house is critical to the success of its design. Any given solution will determine how the house's setting will be experienced and understood by those within. Arches, pediments and simple rustic lintels are amongst the devices used over windows, doors and passageways to add regional flavour and drama to these basic structural forms.

Whether lunettes or ovals, whether multi-paned or sheer, windows can transform mere vistas into carefully choreographed masterpieces. Louvred shutters, curtains and blinds, on the other hand, can add character and mystery. From without, windows reflect water views indoors in the form of transparent glimmer or dramatic, dancing refractions.

Doorways, windows and passages beckon us out of ourselves to interact with the environment. In waterside houses, they set their sights – and focus ours – on their reason for being: to enframe and enhance vistas of lakes, rivers or the sea.

Inland Theatre

The sounds produced by flowing rivers and streams are enchanting, and siting a house beside one of these lively bodies of water can provide a lifetime of magic both visual and aural. The house's precise relationship to the water is key because too much sound can be overpowering and irritating. River water splashes, runs and trickles, and the sounds vary since water levels often change seasonally. Rivers and smaller watercourses are supplied water in several ways, by precipitation, direct overland run-off, springs and seepages, or melting water from snow-fields and glaciers. Typically, a river's existence progresses from perennial through intermittent to ephemeral streams. Ephemeral streams flow only during storms, their channels remaining dry most of the time. Flat-floored trenches called dry arroyos are distinct in form from the v-shaped gullies found in humid areas.

Rivers were crucial in the development of ancient civilizations as the sites of permanent ancestral settlements. Necessity fostered the earliest engineering inventions in the form of dykes, embankments and canals since the fertility of land was dependent on irrigation and flood control. As social structures eventually formed to handle these challenges and achievements of survival, the earliest cities developed along river-banks. Today, many trading ports are situated on rivers, and at least portions of the Amazon and Yangtze are navigable by ocean ships. Rivers supply hydropower for electricity, mills and factories. These facilities and modern urban needs are also handled at riverside locations, and the detrimental effects of pollution upon the environment has had a huge impact on river corridors in particular. The ports, docks and quays of many historic riverside cities have become derelict in recent decades. However, the conservation and rehabilitation of docks, wharves and piers have provided interesting architectural opportunities and unique sites for residential development. Recreational boating has generated a renewed interest in riverside marina communities and has added value to river-front development. Also of interest today is the residential use of ships, canal-boats or pontoon houses that can make the on-river location a permanent habitat.

Waterfalls, like rivers, are things of scenic beauty and inspiration and also provide hydroelectric power. A house built beside a waterfall is the constant audience at a pheonomenal performance of nature. Waterfalls arise in the abrupt, steep formations of river channels that cause the water-flow to drop vertically. A characteristic feature of all waterfalls is the plunge pool or basin – sometimes in a series – etched out of the river channel directly beneath the fall.

Like waterfalls, grottoes are rare. Natural grottoes are caves with still pools fed by springs. During the Renaissance and up until the seventeenth century, grottoes were built to imitate those from Classical times with their mythically significant water sources. Historic Italian, French, German and English gardens as well as contemporary houses and resorts have often included those mossy caverns with rocks, shells and pools.

Edgewater

Hudson River, Tarrytown, New York

Richard H. Jenrette has preserved this classical
Hudson River house, likely designed and built by
Robert Mills. In 1854, Alexander Jackson Davis added
an octagonal library and a berm for the Doric porch
facing the river.

British manor-house living was nobly imitated in many of the early colonies and first states of America. Edgewater, the porticoed Neoclassical residence built in 1820 by the great-grandson of a former Scottish subject, colonialist Robert Livingston, is just such a house. Located on the Hudson River in Upstate New York, the house and its bucolic river setting have been preserved by Richard H. Jenrette, no less a noble lord for his generous preservation of this and five other properties of historic significance, all period houses of the first colonial states. 'This is my favourite place to come during the summers. It has the feeling of a Louisiana bayou,' says Jenrette, who grew up in North Carolina surrounded by great old plantation houses.

Edgewater, situated directly on the banks of the Hudson, enjoys close views of the river in three directions and is unlike other Hudson River residences in its resemblance to Neoclassical mansions of the American South. The house is an excellent example of the American classicism which followed British Palladianism. Most houses of this type had the same pedimented façades and were sited on slight hills overlooking plantations or deer parks with rivers or streams within distant view. Other examples include George Washington's Mt Vernon, Gunston Hall in Lorton, Virginia, and Barker House in Edenton, North Carolina.

In 1852, Edgewater was sold to Robert Donaldson, a retired financier and patron of the arts who had distinguished himself as a landscape designer and tastemaker. Donaldson hired a renowned architect of his day, Alexander Jackson Davis, to add a Gothic octagonal library to the west side of the house. Together, Donaldson and Davis ingeniously added grassed terraces to hide the supporting piers of the portico and turned the river-front façade into a temple with a rolling sweep of lawn leading gently outwards to the surrounding trees and river-bank. Davis advocated the picturesque elements of medievalism. His influence on the distinct classicism of Edgewater was minimal, but it softened the original forms of the building.

Richard Jenrette has continued his preservation and renovation work in the same gentle mode. The regular sequence of the French doors opens the entire front of the house to the portico and view of the river. Six Doric columns of double height support the portico itself, which creates an ample porch for dining with a view of the Hudson – only a stone's throw away. The octagonal library, a favourite retreat of Jenrette, houses several pieces of exquisite mahogany furniture. 'Here I can have multiple views of the river,' he says. 'One is through a group of windows that looks out to the locust trees – as old as the house itself – and to the river with the Catskill Mountains in the background. Another view across the river is framed by the Doric columns of the portico. It's the kind of marvellous combination of architecture and nature which the original Palladian architects sought.' This is a fitting association for Edgewater, bringing the classical grandeur and pastoral setting of England's manor-house traditions to an American river house.

left The dining-room is on axis with a large window view of the Hudson River. An English crystal chandelier from 1830 lights the 1825 Empire dining-room table crafted in New York. The Duncan Phyfe dining chairs belonged to the family of Robert Livingston, an uncle of Edgewater's original owner. The carpet is a late eighteenth-century Aubusson.

below left Fashionable nineteenth-century architect Alexander Davis added the high-ceilinged, one-storey octagonal library in 1854 for his friend Robert Donaldson. It is furnished with Donaldson's own suite of Duncan Phyfe furniture and Jacob Eichholtz's portrait of a child with the background of the Hudson River. 'It is my favourite place to sit and read when the weather is too cool or damp on the front porch,' says Jenrette.

opposite In the drawing-room is a mahogany sofa by Duncan Phyfe with curule legs ending in gilt brass paws. Between the doors to the porch and the river are girandoles crowned with eagles. The pier table is from the Livingston family, the original owners of Edgewater.

opposite On one side of the dining-room is a window bay separated by French doors. It is the end point of an enfilade axis leading from the octagonal library through the drawing-room and dining-room. The sunny, faceted bay window holds a pedestal table with a dolphin base.

above The upstairs bedrooms provide excellent views of the river. 'The proximity to the water makes everything greener,' says Jenrette. 'The river holds warmth so fall comes later here.'

right Richard Jenrette's bedroom has a Federal-period mahogany bed with a reproduction spread and hangings. The house purchase coincided with his decision to collect Federal and Empire furniture. Using Robert Donaldson's 1872 furnishings inventory, Jenrette sought out comparable pieces and bought back numbers of Edgewater's mid- to late nineteenth-century furnishings and paintings.

A Contemporary *Ohana*

Stream and Waterfall, Hawaii Island, Hawaii

Aspen photographer John C. Russell's house was integrated into its five-acre stream-and-ocean site by means of a berm, a shallow, sloped roof and its dark purple colour of Hawaiian lava rock.

t was the element of surprise that prompted photographer John C. Russell to buy a five-acre cliff site on the island of Hawaii. 'When we found the lot, we came upon the *ohana* [guest-house], and I thought, "Why would anyone want to be here?" Then, all of sudden, we heard this noise, went round the house, and there was this bubbling stream. It transformed our whole image of the place.' Perched on the edge of a stream which drops over a cliff into the Pacific Ocean, the site overlooks miles of natural terrain with the distant backdrop of majestic volcanoes sloping down to the coast. Unusually, this part of Hawaii is dry and has an almost desert-like landscape with fountain grasses and low shrubs carpeting ancient lava flows. At this point, too, winds are funnelled between two large volcanoes and across the site. The stream is such a surprise because it is hidden by the rise of the land; the sound it makes is masked by the sounds of the sea.

It was the vastness of the site that first struck architect Andy Neumann. 'The sense of the land is so powerful and compelling that we wanted to make the house disappear and not interrupt the tranquility and vastness,' he says. 'We built a large earth berm which deflects the winds as well as hides the house, adding to the sense of surprise and blending in with the natural landscape.' The house site is separated from the distant fields by the stream. The design evolved naturally by responding to the site conditions. Landscape architect David Tamura carefully retained the natural feeling of the site by using indigenous plantings, and he also suggested that the house be painted a dark colour so that it might appear like a 'shadow' on the landscape and disappear into it. The three-bedroom plan is spread out along the stream and stepped back so that most rooms have views of the waterfall as well as of the volcanoes and ocean. The house turns its back to the wind and opens up to the view and the sun, and on the leeward side, the trellised deck is calm on even the windiest days.

To keep the house simple, the entire roof is comprised of one shallow pitched slope. Once inside, the pine poles which support a flat-roofed exterior portico continue down four one-foot level changes, leading to the prime viewing location perched over the edge of the stream and peering down on the waterfall. The eight-by-ten-foot picture windows are canted outwards to emphasize the same view. 'We recaptured the element of surprise,' explains Russell, 'as you move from the entrance court, softened by the landscaping and trees, then step down the first slab at the entrance and descend to the second slab of the kitchen–dining area and end at the lowest living-room level with the windows tilting out, revealing the waterfall.' The natural slate counter tops and fireplace facing link the house to the site. Combined with the berm structure, the natural-coloured materials for wall, roof and floor all add to the sense of being grounded to the rocky stream below.

The straightforward materials and relaxed forms create a comfortable vacation environment. Although the design consciously avoided trying to look like any particular style, the peeled pine logs, low roof, louvred vents and open glass side make the house appear like an indigenous *ohana* pavilion set close to the water.

left *Ohana* means 'family' in Hawaiian; the term also refers to a simple family guesthouse. The house's peeled pine logs, low roof and strong indoor–outdoor relationship relate it to the vernacular *ohana*. Inside, the main living spaces have an open plan, and the pine poles step down the site through four one-foot level changes.

above 'We recaptured the element of surprise,' says Russell, 'as you descend through the house.' The plan of the house follows the stream and steps back so that most of the rooms have views of the waterfall and ocean.

right The high ceiling of the master bedroom shows the open transoms connecting the room with other spaces under the continuous roof span. The canopy bed is covered with an Oriental patterned spread.

Mosse Tea-House

Kilfane Glen and Waterfall, Kilkenny County, Ireland

A 1790s Romantic-period 'cottage orné' nestles in a ravine, poised at the edge of a Kilkenny County stream and waterfall. Originally built by Sir John and Lady Power, it has been rebuilt by present owners Susan and Nicholas Mosse.

'The entire site is as special as the waterfall,' says Susan Mosse, describing Kilfane Glen and Waterfall, part of the grounds of the estate in County Kilkenny, Ireland, where she and her husband, Nicholas, have rebuilt an eighteenth-century tea-house. 'It is nestled in a small ravine, closed on both sides with beautiful rock-faced cliffs and towering trees planted in the eighteenth century,' she continues. 'A longish winding path leading to it creates a feeling of passage, of tunnelling into somewhere new.'

The garden at Kilfane House was originally laid out during the 1790s by Sir John and Lady Power, members of south-eastern Ireland's intelligentsia. The tea-house was the Powers' cottage orné, a picturesque element strategically placed on the edge of their property. Sir John Power diverted water from a stream into a small canal to flow over a rocky cliff beside the cottage orné.

The Mosses discovered some wall and floor remains of the original structure, although shrubbery growth had caused the waterfall to cease flowing. After finding the original sketches for the cottage orné, they embarked on its restoration and that of the gardens and waterfall, receiving assistance from the European Union garden restoration scheme.

Now the pool at the base of the fall once again extends into a small channel which joins the main stream nearby. West of the fall is a grotto – one destination of a stone stairway leading up the cliff from the ravine. The tea-house itself is enchanting. Ferns, aquilegias and salvias are planted in beds along its walls, and honeysuckle grows at the front door. The structure includes an octagonal drawing-room with a fireplace, a small kitchen, a bedroom suite and a small vestibule looking out towards the moss-covered cliff and tree-trunks. David Sheehan of Sheehan & Barry helped in the rebuilding, and even the cobbled paving was restored. Thatcher Matt Phelan imported reeds from Norfolk since they were no longer available in the area.

'The original designers in the eighteenth century certainly knew what they were doing, and the slightly askew placement of the house vis-à-vis the waterfall is perfect, as are the "morning" porch and "evening" porch, which have separate views and sound qualities,' says Susan Mosse. 'All seasons are best for such wilderness dwelling,' Nicholas Mosse adds. His wife even finds winter there remarkable. 'Perhaps because snow is so rare in Ireland, I particularly love it when ice and snow cover everything and all the songbirds cluster around the flowing water,' she says. 'We also have a special bird called a dipper, and a pair of them make their home in the middle of the fall, behind the water.' Susan Mosse feels that the remoteness and peace of the place have given her a keener appreciation of nature. 'The funny thing about waterfalls is that they just keep falling,' she says. 'There is a gentle roar associated with ours, and some people love this noise – like my husband – and some people have trouble sleeping nearby – alas, like myself. We use the tea-house for guests and parties mainly, and I think the ionized air generated by the waterfall creates a heady atmosphere, which makes even the most exhausted, grumpiest person relax and smile.'

opposite On one side of the octagonal drawing-room is a fireplace and twiggy overmantel displaying the 'cottage-orné' plates designed and made by Nicholas Mosse at his pottery. The Irish chair dates from the first quarter of the nineteenth century.

right Cross-muntin windows and French doors hung with white calico curtains form three walls of the octagonal tea-room and provide views of the waterfall. A round table set for tea is attended by two nineteenth-century chairs. David Sheehan of Sheehan & Barry helped to rebuild the cottage with architectural historian Jeremy Williams, who found the early sketches of the garden structure.

below The twig table and seats on the small rear terrace, as well as the fences, were made of forest thinnings by Pat Butler. The small vestibule looks towards the moss-covered cliff.

Palm Pavilions

Capibaribe River Waterfalls, Viçosa, Brazil

Constructed of indigenous palms and stones, architect Gerson Castelo Branco's house overlooks seven falls in a wildlife preserve in Brazil's Ceará Province. Its rooms open to the forest and resonate with the sounds of water.

'It is my "Paraqueira Brasileira", my paradise,' says architect Gerson Castelo Branco of his year-round home, located in the jungles of Brazil's Ceará Province near Viçosa. The Capibaribe River runs through the eighty-acre property and is enlivened by no fewer than seven waterfalls. 'Both the river and the forest attract particular birds and wildlife to the site because it's really their habitat,' says Branco. 'My area is a forest preserve, and I don't allow hunting, so the animals favour it because they feel safe here.'

In harmony with the wildlife, Branco's home is also at one with the physical elements at an altitude of two thousand feet on the plateau of the Ibiapaba Sierra. 'I put the house on the highest place of the site so it would be possible to see the first waterfall,' he says. 'But I preserved some distance to the fall because of the excessive moisture and noise of the rushing water during the rainy season. The water's sound is always present in the house, but it's very quiet.'

Using indigenous materials, Branco built the house with pillars fashioned from carnauba-palm trunks and wall panels of herringbone-patterned palm stems. Slender cane-like sticks arranged in rows cover the ceilings and some of the walls. Floors are of slate or rough-cut planks covered with straw matting. The house is a small compound composed of two structures: a main house of three storeys with a jutting triangulated roof; a smaller structure of two storeys located a few steps up from the main house's ground floor; and a covered porch between the two. Branco takes breakfast and lunch on the porch, where he can be with the birds and wild animals. While the main house contains the living-room, master bedroom and guest bedrooms, the second house contains the dining-room, kitchen, a home office and servants' quarters.

The double-height interior of the main house is a lofty space revealing the ground- and first-floor living areas with hammocks and day-beds for lounging. A central staircase curves upwards to the first-floor sleeping quarters, which are draped, four-poster chambers called *camarinhas*, almost like desert campaign tents. Branco's master bedroom is also on the first floor. It is a spacious open area with an ample observation deck from which the architect can listen to the nearest waterfall. 'The forest and the first waterfall are seen here as well as through the glass panels of every opening of the house,' he says. 'The house is all transparent to the river.' Branco's house is site-specific and works well with the regional climate and ecological concerns.

'I want my houses to show that it is possible to live in a unique way,' he says. While Brazilian modernists Roberto Burle-Marx and Oscar Niemeyer produced hard-edged, geometric structures of concrete and steel, Branco prefers the 'native' style of palm wood-and-stone houses, made from the natural resources of the country.

'This house isn't a weekend house; it's my home,' says Branco. The architect often works here, though he also keeps an office in Ceará's capital city of Fortaleza. 'I stay here for long seasons when the clients permit it, of course. However, Brazil is a big place, and my architectural work takes me to many regions. But I am forever happy when returning to my paradise.'

above Colourful local fabrics drape the upper-floor sleeping quarters, which are four-poster chambers called *camarinhas*.

right Branco's home is on one of the highest points of the plateau of the Ibiapaba Sierra. 'I preserved some distance to the fall because of the excessive moisture and noise of the rushing water during the rainy season,' he says.

opposite top An alcove for watching television, located in the first-floor living-room, gives the feeling of a tree house with its view to the palms, hammock and treetops.

opposite bottom left One corner of the kitchen holds a credenza with palm-stem panels and shelves built into the wall behind. Baskets and regional crafts are interspersed with personal objects and memorabilia.

opposite bottom right Perched high in the second pavilion where the soothing sounds of the waterfall are quiet but constant, the home office is furnished with a desk piled with books, small sculptures and geological finds.

left A crystal is placed at the exact centre of the main pavilion, on the post of the first-storey landing. The jutting triangulated roof creates the soaring space of the double-height interior. Large double door frames open to a pair of terraces. Floors are of wooden planks.

opposite top left Indigenous palm stems and fronds were woven and crafted to create structural and decorative objects throughout the house. Walls and doors made of palm stems surround a built-in desk and shelves with baskets in the master suite.

opposite top right The two-storey structure under the triangulated roof holds the home office, kitchen and servants' quarters. Stone piers and the palm-trunk frame create a shaded porch under the terrace.

opposite left The angled roof over the main structure shows a broad panel of palm stems to shade and enclose the upper-storey master bedroom. Along the ground-floor living-room is a wood-rail terrace pointing out towards the forest and the sounds of the nearest waterfall.

opposite right Interior and exterior spaces are intertwined, and the central spiral staircase shows the transparent frame of the house through which another stair located on the far wall of the ground floor, left, leads outdoors.

Casa Akle

Lake, Cliffs and Mountains, Valle de Bravo, Mexico

Casa Akle was designed by architect Ricardo Legorreta to focus on the spectacular lake and virgin landscape of a Mexican colonial town. The house's angled roofs and mustard-hued walls mimic the rocky cliffs, while interiors are accented with Bougainvillaea colours.

Ricardo Legorreta has designed many structures by the sea, as well as houses incorporating man-made pools, for which he is world-renowned. Especially famous are the Camino Real hotels which terrace down to the Gulf of Mexico at Ixtapa and Cancun. 'I feel that the major elements of Mexican architecture which I impart to my work are walls, water and earth colours,' says the architect, who has offices in Mexico City and Los Angeles, California.

Mexico is known for its sensual coastal settings, so when Legorreta was asked in the mid-1990s to design a home for a lake-front community, he felt it would be an unusual challenge and an opportunity to create a different experience of water. 'The house is at a wooded location along the Valle de Bravo's lake shore, and the terrain has a very steep slope with spectacular views to the lake, as well as a big rock cliff at the back of the house,' explains Legorreta about the site, located in a wooded setting in a colonial city and resort area about two hours south-west of Mexico City.

'The design was planned to adapt itself to the different ground levels, trying to avoid, as much as possible, the use of big structures,' the architect observes. 'We were inspired by the local popular architecture to use angled roofs, referred to as "scope" roofs.' These roofs are a response to the rainy conditions in this area surrounding a lake; other building materials, most of them local, were used with ease of maintenance in mind. They include local rocks and concrete for the floors, fibreglass for the doors, and oxide-based paint to resist wear. The exterior walls are painted a mustard colour which reflects the hue of the Valle de Bravo cliffs as well as the red of the tile roofs and terracotta terrace paving.

Meant to seem small, the house is a perfect size for the couple for whom it was designed. 'For the interiors, the idea was to maintain a sparse, nearly empty appearance by emphasizing the spaces rather than the decorative elements,' says Legorreta. Art objects were placed at key locations, and the final effect is very elegant, even though the style throughout is informal. Simply furnished, the high-ceilinged interior spaces reflect the forms of the sloped roofs, and the built-in natural wood cabinets found throughout create a sense of decoration with their architectonic grid patterns. In the living area, lustrous wood floors and beams define the space. Along one wall, a recessed wall is painted a vivid melon colour; above it is a gridded studio window which allows light to wash gently over the space.

A corner of one bedroom offers a cozy yet clean-lined design with low, square-mullioned windows framed by window seats below and a drop soffit above. The windows frame the wrap-around view across the lake to distant mountains. However, the best views of the lake are from the terraces, where the angled roofs follow the shape of the cliff and lead to the water. Windows cut through the terrace walls frame different views. The combination of concrete columns, terracotta and stone paving, angled walls, gridded windows and wood-beamed porches make the terraces appear modern yet traditional, while the view appears ancient with its deep blue, still waters and uninhabited mountains.

opposite top left For the interiors, Legorreta emphasized the spaces rather than the decorative details. 'The idea was to maintain a sparse, nearly empty appearance which would be informal and casual,' he says. The high-ceilinged living-room area is detailed with wooden beams, a corner fireplace, a recessed rose-coloured wall and a gridded studio window.

opposite top right The dining area is continuous with the living-room and is furnished with an oblong table surrounded by ladderback cane chairs painted a colourful purple. Built-in natural wood shelves have grid-patterned cabinet doors.

opposite bottom left Valle de Bravo Lake and the distant mountains are the focus of the master bedroom, seen through low, square-mullioned windows. Simply furnished, the room is dramatically accented with a purple carpet and an angled-beam ceiling.

opposite bottom right Steep steps and a louvred baffle are the structural elements which create the interior decoration of the guest-room, which is provided with three beds.

right The rustic shape of the red stone cliff is juxtaposed with the smooth mustard colour of the house. Like a terraced cliff, the stepped configuration of the house forms a broad terrace at the lowest level of the house, where large willow-and-pigskin Equipale chairs surround the fireplace of the roofed outdoor living-room.

Wood on the Water

Widely available, pliable, resilient and easily stainable, wood has been an essential building material for millennia. Since trees have always grown in abundance at waterside locations, dwellings built there frequently feature wood's special qualities, sometimes showcasing the influence of local boat- and shipbuilding crafts.

Wood is the staple of innumerable modern building types, providing cladding, structural support and a huge range of decorative motifs. One notable seaside example is the Shingle Style, one of the first indigenous domestic styles in America. The naturalism of nobly weathered Shingle-Style exteriors have inspired modern architects to evolve exciting, sometimes startling variations of this American perennial. Elsewhere, designers have exploited as many different variations on the themes of grain, pattern and texture as can be imagined, creating inspirational curves, grids and modules to make the most of wood's integral relationship with waterside environments the world over.

Island Hideaways

slands cast a magic spell on our imaginations as they separate us from the rest of the world, creating their own worlds in seemingly infinite oceans. Because of their isolation, islands can foster habits and customs which are entirely distinct from those of neighbouring landmasses, as can be seen on the Galapagos and Madagascar. As a result, islands make admirable vacation retreats, but those who settle on them and build houses must be adventurous and independent and love isolation. The actor Marlon Brando, who spent years on his own Tahitian island, comes to mind.

One of the most distinctive land–sea patterns is the graceful sweep of an island arc, a long, curved chain of islands. There are twenty-two of these on earth. Island arcs were formed when large, laterally rigid plates of the earth's surface moved about relative to one another. Volcanism also formed island arcs, as in the case of Hawaii. Most arc-associated volcanoes are found in the so-called 'circle of fire' which rings the Pacific Ocean and extends into the Atlantic, with one arc ringing the Caribbean and the other, the Scotia Sea. Many buildable islands do not belong to arcs and are simply rifts in lakes or rivers or extensions of continental land. They range in size from the small scale of the Ile de la Cité in the River Seine in Paris to the continental scale of Australia, from tiny uninhabited islands of the Pacific to crowded Manhattan.

Historically, islands have provided ideal locations for houses and palatial structures which continue to inspire. The Roman Emperor Hadrian's colonnaded theatre provided both a means of escape and a source of entertainment. Mont-St-Michel provided a place of refuge. Isola Bella, on an island in Lake Maggiore in Italy, was constructed in the seventeenth century as a pleasure villa with garden parterres and a Baroque theatre dominating the hundred-foot-high terrace.

Islands are popular in Oriental cultures as sites for shrines and temples since their isolation can express spiritual detachment. Chinese and Japanese islands are often man-made features supporting pavilions in lakes and ponds. Tanah Lot, a temple in Bali, stands dramatically on a small island composed of a single massive rock. It is connected to a larger island by a low-lying sand flat which is filled with saltwater pools most of the time.

While island isolation has been used as a punishment, as in the case of Napoleon's exile to the island of St Helena or the emprisonment of criminals at Alcatraz in California, a connection with water is normally one of the pleasures of island living. This connection is most beneficial when people are allowed to get as close to the water as possible. The most important design element of a waterside house is its relationship to the water; islands can provide a 360-degree view and offer many opportunities for tangible appreciation of the water's edge.

Palermo Coast Arches

Gulf of Solanto, Sicily, Italy

Textured tufa and classical details inspired by the island's ancient structures are blended in the multi-level house Antonio D'Andrea designed for a family along Sicily's craggy and wooded Palermo Coast.

A house located close to one of Sicily's most beautiful bodies of water, the Gulf of Solanto, is surrounded by vegetation and has a most evocative sea view from its terrace. 'For the design of the house, we wanted to make sure that it did not look like a new construction but like a restoration of something which already existed, similar to the local historic architecture, which is immersed in nature,' says architect Antonio D'Andrea, who designed the house with partner Ignacio Mallol.

Not many miles east of Palermo, the area is rich in ancient structures from the pre-Christian era. One nearby city, Punich, has cobbled streets as well as Hellenistic and Roman houses with wall paintings. 'Like the region's ancient structures, the house is not an isolated block, but is meant to be like a little village of the region's ancient structures,' D'Andrea explains. 'Many elements of the house are connected to one another with arched passages which join the central house to the sides as well as to stone stairs which descend into the vegetation,' D'Andrea continues. 'We used local materials, especially the golden-yellow tufa stone from the seventeenth century, which was hand-worked by a restorer for the exterior of the house. For the interior walls, an encaustic material was used which gives the sensation of old walls stained by time, weather and the salt air.'

Realized on diverse levels, the plan of the house focuses primarily on the salon on the upper floor. The room's façade, formed of three arches crowned with two volutes, creates a large porch which opens the house to the terrace overlooking the sea. A gazebo offers a table and chairs to rest or dine by the water, and a big pine tree – saved during construction – appears like an umbrella, protecting the outdoor lounging area. During the evenings, the area is illuminated by bronze lanterns.

The interiors emanate a sense of the Antique. There is painted Sicilian furniture from the seventeenth century, including a wooden table simulating a stack of books, and local sixteenth-century and contemporary earthenware and ceramic vases. In addition to the colours of the tufa walls and terracotta flooring, the predominant hues of the interiors are of coral and tropical fruit. 'Walnut beams give the high ceilings a sense of lightness and total fusion with the trees outside,' says D'Andrea. 'Another attempt to make the inside appear like the outside is the large arched window in the master bedroom which opens to the pool area.' Bordered in tufa, the pool was designed in the irregular shape of the inlet below the house. From the house, it seems like a step towards the sea; it is located near the rocks, so that from certain aspects the two seem to be parts of each other.

'You can live here year-round because of the favourable climate,' observes D'Andrea. 'The sea is limpid blue without strong currents, and it is so warm that it makes swimming very pleasurable. In this place, the local perfume of lemons and mandarins is intoxicating, and there is the sensation of quietness and well-being. Because of the ancient and timeless character of the place, you can nearly imagine the mythical Ulysses sailing by on the waters of the beautiful Gulf of Solanto.'

opposite top The main terrace offers a view of the Gulf of Solanto and the distant Sicilian hills, and it is furnished with a seventeenth-century Sicilian well planted with waterlillies. An elaborate sunburst is represented in the paving.

opposite bottom left One corner of the terrace features a tented gazebo over a pedestal dining table. Chairs are upholstered in a casual stripe like the tent. During the evenings, the area is illuminated by the bronze lanterns.

opposite bottom right The interiors, which D'Andrea creataed in collaboration with interior designer Leonardo Tognoni, represent the Sicilian merging of earthy and ornate elements. The base of the dining table is gnarled wood.

above From the gabled wooden living-room ceiling hangs a contemporary Sicilian wooden sculpture. The amply scaled room is furnished with large plush seating, swagged curtains and a rich mix of upholstery and carpet patterns.

left Grand wicker chairs flank the entrance to the house through the grotto-like, low Roman arches of the porch, which overlooks the Gulf. On axis with the tufa-faced entrance is the stone living-room fireplace, showing an age-old, curved Sicilian form.

above A vaulted passage with a marble capital leads to one bedroom facing the water. 'The large arched window and the terracotta paving make the bedroom appear like it is a part of the terrace outside,' D'Andrea explains.

Camp Fiddlehead

Penobscot Bay, Vinalhaven Island, Maine

Susan Rodriguez and Charles Lowrey's house is designed as shed-roof structures camped out on a bluff on their own eight-acre island. When shrouded in fog, the cabin loses all contact with the bay, except for the ever-present sound of fog horns.

Vinalhaven, an island in Penobscot Bay twelve miles off the coast of Maine, is covered with hemlock and spruce trees. Lobster pots are stacked in each of its residents' backyards. Having summered on the remote island since 1981, architect Susan Rodriguez and her husband, Charles Lowrey, fell in love with a tiny adjacent island called Fiddlehead. After coaxing its owners to sell the eight-acre site, they built a cabin on a bluff to take advantage of the island's sight-lines. Decks and large windows now face the summer sunsets and look out over a narrow channel busy with picturesque boats.

'The overall house is composed of two simple shed-roof cabins joined by a raised deck and walkway,' explains Rodriguez, who, as a principal of James Stewart Polshek & Partners in New York, rarely designs such small structures. 'The larger cabin opens up to the water view and the smaller one to the wooded landscape. The natural weathering of the wooden structures will further integrate them into the natural setting.' Using vernacular construction methods and materials and following her own sensitivity to the natural environment, Rodriguez designed post-and-beam hemlock volumes clad in cedar shingles with a laminated pine deck between the two cabins. Asphalt shingles cover the steeply angled shed roofs. All building materials were brought by barge to the site at high tide, including the cedar trim and the pine shutters which face the deck. These large shutters are actually sliding barn doors which can fully enclose the house during storms. They slide on barn-door tracks and are crossed by tension rods made at the local

boatyard. Small wooden shutters swing upwards on the other windows. The wedge-shaped deck of laminated pine located between the cabins is a casual outdoor living-room where teak deck chairs provide an opportunity to soak up a bit of midday sun. On the west, at the widest end of the wedged deck, stairs expand outwards to a sloped field, inviting one into the woods.

'I designed a continuous clerestory window in the main cabin to disengage the sloping roof from the vertical wall surface. Its effect is an unusual visual penetration of interior to exterior,' explains Rodriguez. The larger cabin holds the living–dining areas with bedrooms on two levels. In the late afternoons, a golden light filters into the main living–dining-room from the rafters and creates a dance of shadows on the slanting planes of the wooden ceiling. Below, walls are surfaced in laminated ponderosa-pine decking in the span between the clerestory window and the large deck windows, which allow views across the deck to the narrow channel. The smaller cabin is a guest-house with flexible space for recreation. Laminated decking is once again the surfacing material here, between the timber posts and trusses of the exposed post-and-beam structure. The cabins' decor is practical and based on camping imagery.

This island retreat is totally self-sufficient: water comes from a well and rain collected from the roof; a small generator pumps the water; propane powers the appliances and lighting; a wood-burning stove provides heat when necessary. 'At times, we're stranded there by the weather, but it's all part of the challenge of island living,' says Rodriguez.

opposite above left
Referencing a simpler era, an oak Craftsman rocker provides a warm and comfortable seat beside the living-room's pot-belly stove. 'My design was inspired by basic utilitarian buildings – a fisherman's shack and a bunkhouse – which were on the site,' says architect Susan Rodriguez.

opposite above right
Vernacular construction methods and natural materials were used in the main cabin holding the living-room and kitchen areas. The walls are surfaced in laminated ponderosa-pine decking, and the large windows look out over a deck to a narrow, busy channel.

opposite below left The steeply angled shed roof and its open construction create dramatic spaces in the large main cabin, which holds the living–dining areas and bedrooms. In the late afternoons, light from the clerestory windows filters into the space through the upper beams.

opposite below right The guest cabin is another shed-roof structure with timber posts and trusses displaying the basic post-and-beam construction. It is decorated with practical camp objects: four oars and a striped, wool camp blanket.

right The cabin is sited on the mossy north side of the island. 'You are incredibly aware of being on a small island where there are different ecosystems depending upon the orientation,' says Rodriguez. 'While the south side is windblown, open and grassy, the north side is very green, with boulders and moss among spruce and fir trees.'

An Amanpuri Eyrie

Gulf of Siam, Phuket, Thailand

The uppermost level of Edward Tuttle's beach-side compound on a Phuket peninsula displays a pool and Thai pavilion like those at nearby Amanpuri, the renowned hotel he designed a decade earlier, based on Ayudthya-period temples.

'Living in nature and being surrounded by water and the gardens are spoiling,' says American-born, Paris-based designer Edward Tuttle. Tuttle lives as many months of the year as possible at his home on Phuket Island. 'The style of life, the Thai way, is both subtle and rich. It is gracious like the Thai people in their mannerisms and their kindness.'

Tuttle's work is synonymous with contemporary Thailand, although he has also worked throughout Asia, particularly in Hong Kong and Singapore, and in Indonesia, especially in Bali. He uses a defined geometry which respects regional forms and adapts local building materials wherever he works. In this way, he returns to the time-honoured techniques of indigenous architecture. Because of their lush tropical settings, Tuttle's projects are considered landscaping solutions as much as architectural ones, and he will often design the furniture for a house as well. After he finished the Amanpuri Hotel on Phuket, Tuttle started his own house on the peninsula of the hotel property. The site is an excellent one, considered one of the most beautiful on Phuket. The house hangs on the cliff, and the water is about sixty-five feet away from the lowest structures. 'Hanging on the cliff, the house is all about water. It is surrounded by water,' says Tuttle.

A beach-side compound, the house is made up of a cluster of tropical pavilions. 'The house is based on temple architecture of the Ayudthya period, from the fifteenth to the eighteenth century. It is the most beautiful period of Thai architecture,' Tuttle observes. Different pavilions rest on the uppermost slab, which is about 50 feet wide by 250 feet long. A pool is suspended from that slab as well. Then, Tuttle explains, 'there are staircases going down to different levels connected to the land and suspended by columns off the ground.' Below the first slab, terracing down the hill in local fashion, there is another level, and then, at the third level down, yet another slab, which is also 50 by 250 feet, just as large as the uppermost slab. The pavilions are havens of tranquility, providing structural unity but also functional flexibility, privacy as well as openness. Forming bedrooms, open-air salons and dining spaces, they are covered with thatched roofs held up by wooden posts.

'We are constantly aware of the water and the gardens,' Tuttle concludes. 'Our house is on a peninsula, but we are at a point where the peninsula is very narrow, so we have the view of the water from both sides. And since it is a compound of elements spread out with gardens separating the structures, you never really have the whole idea of what it constitutes unless you experience it. The combination of the vastness of the water views and the lushness of the garden setting is quite incredible.'

left A staircase leads from the upper level to a decorative viewing pavilion which is both connected to the land and suspended above it on slender columns.

opposite above Surrounded entirely by glass doors, the living-room pavilion can be entirely opened or closed to protect it from the cool evenings. Seating is created from banquettes which step down into the room. Edward Tuttle used indigenous woods and defined geometric forms which respect regional shapes and yet appear modern.

opposite below The stone-paved dining-room becomes a casual garden room. The wooden post and drop soffit support a lofty roof.

left Tuttle has worked throughout South-east Asia for thirty years, and his work has forged a contemporary Thai style. His master bedroom shows the simple geometry and interrelationship with nature characteristic of his work. The room is based on a square with openings to the tropical gardens on a cross axis. The sculptures are from the Ayudthya period.

top One airy guest bedroom features built-ins and the contemporary cane chairs found throughout the compound house, which were designed by Tuttle.

above The central axial openings of the master bedroom provide focused views to the terraces, tropical gardens and gulf waters. The design takes full advantage of the narrow peninsula, which provides broad views of the water from both sides.

Sardinia Point Paradise

Bonifacio Straits, Sardinia, Italy

Sardinia is an island paradise with one particularly beautiful location overlooking a calm bay and tiny group of islands. The house architect Alberto Ponis designed here, set against a rocky ridge, is barely discernable from its surroundings.

'Close contact with nature in this extraordinary and untouched environment is the dominant theme in my architecture, where the natural constraints are a constant source of inspiration,' explains architect Alberto Ponis about his design for this house. 'The house is sited at Punta Sardegna near the small town of Palau and opposite the island group of La Maddalena,' he continues. 'It is located in the north of Sardinia, separated from Corsica by the Bonifacio Straits, a very windy and narrow stretch of water in the centre of the Mediterranean Sea. But in spite of the strong western wind, called the mistral, the coast of Punta Sardegna, facing east, is well protected, and the water in front of the house is calm.'

Seen from land or sea, this house is barely discernable from its surroundings. It is situated against a rocky ridge, and its volume follows that of these large granite masses. The walls were plastered using the traditional trowel technique, and their warm beige colour echoes that of the rocks. The fan-shaped plan provides each space with a view, while sensitive window placement defines picture-perfect vistas of the tranquil sea and the tiny islands of La Maddalena.

However organic the design, it is also very contemporary, with walls of prefabricated concrete and roofs held up by exposed beams arranged in a fan to follow the plan of the house. Roof tiles also follow its overall shape. The kitchen is the only room with a flat roof, which is used as a terrace, accessible by an outside brick staircase.

The landscape has been left in its natural state, all rocks and earth with native *macchia mediterranea*, shrubs and low trees, particularly the *arbuitus grove*. Terraces fit into the spaces left by the rock formations, and between the rocks, pathways lead down to the beach and provide secret places to view the coast.

Living spaces extend outdoors with brick-paved terraces and patios at ground level. One terrace provides a place for al fresco dining with an outdoor oven and fireplace. Another is actually the entrance to the house, appearing casual and half-hidden by the rocks and plantings when seen from a distance. Thus, each outdoor space is an extension of the house, and the house opens itself up by means of wide glass doors which offer panoramic vistas. It benefits from being at one with its unique island site, protected from harsh weather and endowed with terrain which is beautiful in all seasons.

opposite A close connection to nature is key to Ponis's design, and one terrace for al fresco dining includes a palm-and-log canopy and a rock island in the middle of the swimming pool. 'I respect the ancient granite formations of sculptural forms and the wild spontaneous vegetation,' says the architect.

right Wide sliding doors open the living-room to one terrace, making it an extension of the space. White canvas sofas and outdoor cane chairs create a continuous conversation grouping.

right Local folk arts influence the informal interior dining area. A 'fish' weather vane and cane café chairs furnish the space, and an arched window, wood-panelled door and decorated dado reflect building crafts of the area.

opposite Draperies of the
canopy bed in the master
bedroom frame a large window
view of a seemingly untouched
island environment, with the
primitive palm-and-log
sunscreen, rock formations,
sea vista and La Maddalena
island group.

above The plan provides each
space with a view and a terrace,
and another bedroom shares
a picture-perfect image of the
water. Vines cover the support
for the outdoor hammock.

right A lacy Sardinian hammock
hangs from the exposed wooden
beams of one porch where vines
and granite mesh with the
structure of the house.

Palm and Coral Huts

Polynesian Lagoon, Tahiti, South Pacific

French architect Jean-Claude Michel designed his own lagoon home as a group of three primitive huts raised above the water. The structures are made from palm trunks and leaves with coral footings and roofs of thatch and fibre shingles.

'I love to live in the greatest possible intimacy with nature and to work in the waves with the coral,' says Jean-Claude Michel about living on Tahiti in French Polynesia. The house he has imaginatively crafted for himself and his family is a set of tiny nest-like structures in a lagoon refuge. The compound of three small structures is located on one of the blue lagoons edging the island. Each structure is hand-crafted like an archaic, organic sculpture or an irrational wonder of nature for a Robinson Crusoe-style paradise.

'At the beginning, my work was Tahitian-style, but here people build things to last for only two to five years before they let them go to the termites,' says Michel. 'I tried this, but now the things I build are constructed to last for a long time. My work has evolved into something a bit stronger and not so local as it used to be.' Palm-trunk piles with coral footings hold up the raised platforms of his huts. Their roofs are thatched with a froth of palm leaves and fibre shingles. Branches twist into odd positions, lending support to the walls. Woven palm leaves, which cover many of the wall surfaces, form frames around windows and doors. For the walls and framework of the house, local blond woods were sculpted into curved shelves and built-in tables, seats and beds. Plexiglass fills many of the irregularly shaped windows, and the only elements which are straight are the boards of the floors and decks.

The tree-house-scaled huts seem to step out into the blue lagoon. In this lush setting, the leafy branches of trees reach down to the clear water whilst also embracing the huts. Michel and his family live in this isolated location populated only by fish, birds and small animals and surrounded by coconut palms, pandamus, lantana, hibiscus and tropical fruit trees. 'Nature offers the sensation of renewing ourselves,' says Michel, who moved to Tahiti from Brittany. 'When I was a child, I had a passion for fishing which developed into this symbiosis with the natural elements. Now, it impels me to such a degree that humanity actually seems to be made up of extra-terrestrials.'

In fact, most Tahitians are terrestrial, nature-loving Polynesians with some French and Chinese in their backgrounds. Easterly trade-winds engulf their island, which was discovered by the British in 1767, then settled by the French later on. One of the Iles du Vent, or Windward Group, Tahiti is divided into a wet south and a dry north, and is a mere thirty-three miles long. The terrain, which comprises two ancient eroded volcanic cones connected by an isthmus, is mountainous and has numerous swift streams. Many coral reefs and lagoons, like Michel's, fringe the jagged coast.

'I left Europe like a rat leaving a sinking ship,' says Michel. His decision to abandon modern society parallels that of his countryman Paul Gauguin, who also settled on Tahiti. 'My life here is like a protest,' he adds. 'It is to show everyone that Tahiti is a tolerant, peaceful Far West where one dares to dream. I could no longer depart from it or from my hut. The Pacific, with the ever-present grand ocean above the coral reef, gives me energy for life.'

above left Michel's three structures all have solid, water-resistant coral footings. The bedroom hut, entered over a bridge of local tree-trunks, has coral walls and an entrance porch covered with palm thatch.

above right The middle fibre-shingled structure shows the tree-house scale of the huts, which step out into the lagoon. Palm trunks create the frame for the large plexiglass window.

left The lagoon is viewed from the large windows of the middle structure. Inside the huts, local woods are sculpted into curved shelves and built-in furnishings. 'My work has evolved into something which is not so much Tahitian as it is personal,' says Michel.

opposite The third hut features a thatched roof and a small terrace with a stick balcony. In this primitive island lagoon, one of Michel's children plays in the shallow water where the leafy branches nearly reach down to the clear water.

All along the Watch-Tower

Pregonda Coast, Menorca, Spain

A turn-of-the-century stone tower and rocky hillside inspired the terraced Menorca Island house Barcelona architect Javier Barba designed with Alfredo Vives. The house has steps leading down to a sandy beach and sequestered cove.

When seen at a distance, this house near Pregonda on the island of Menorca in Spain disappears into the craggy hillside. This effect was planned by Barcelona architect Javier Barba, who designed the house with Alfredo Vives for a European financier and his family. The site is on a steep promontory above a sequestered cove on the wild northern coast of the island. 'It is a marvellous rocky hillside which descends to a private beach and a protected bay, and it is truly one of the most spectacular spots on the Mediterranean, one that many environmental groups are anxious to protect,' says Barba. 'In Menorca, the vernacular architecture is mostly simple, white-washed structures. However, it happens that there is another Menorcan vernacular, an ancient one. For this island was settled in prehistoric times by a people who lived in the island's many caves and built numerous stone megaliths. It was from this that I drew my inspiration, as well as from a rather severe, square-shaped tower which already existed on the site,' Barba explains.

The new house was planned at a forty-five-degree angle to this turn-of-the-century watch-tower and some deteriorating buildings on the lot, incorporating them into the plan. Barba's final design consists of a compound of living areas, including a main house, a pool terrace and a guest-house built into the hillside. 'I envisioned a stone building connected to the tower which would have a powerful, primordial shape – in this case, several stone walls slanting outwards –

and which would be able to hold its own against the drama of the landscape,' says the architect. All of the structures are covered with rocks excavated from the site which give the house continuity with the landscape. Four buttresses counter the building's strong horizontal. The south-east façade includes the pool terrace and the kitchen, dining- and living-room windows, which all look out to sea. Pockets of light and shade are produced by the windows, buttresses and recesses. The roof line of the guest-house, located above the main house, unites with the mountain. The guest-house is roofed with used tiles and decorated with wooden shutters typical of the English colonial influence on the island.

Barba planned that vistas within each space would include a generous view of the cove: 'By orientating the house towards the east, I was able to maximize the views and ensure that the sun hit the house at an angle at which its rays were least intense. I also placed an atrium deep within the interior of the house. This enclosed court brings in natural light, so that the interior is not dark, and provides cross-ventilation.' Terraces, stone paths and gardens are planted with cactuses, cypress trees, lavender and yellow wildflowers indigenous to the cove. Creepers overtake the walls of the roof-top terrace. 'From the terrace, the distance between the house and the edge of the cliff and the view to the water gives the sensation of being perched amongst the rocks and exposed to the elements,' says Barba. 'Reduced to its essence, the house is all about a clear broad sky, a pacific sea and a brutal outcropping of rock.'

opposite top The old watch-tower rises from the roof terrace of the house, which follows the lines of the hillside and is surfaced with stones excavated from the site. Indigenous cypress trees, lavender and wildflowers create the landscaping. Creepers grow over the walls of the roof-top terrace, and the house's angled buttresses separate large glass doors opening the kitchen and dining- and living-rooms to the terrace and pool.

opposite bottom left Mediterranean views are visible through the unmullioned windows and doors located at one end of the living-room where the curved built-in seating faces a raised stone-surfaced fireplace.

opposite bottom right Furnished with the same spare built-in furnishings, the guest-house – built into the hillside – is defined by beamed ceilings, interior stone walls and arched doorways.

above A screen of slender wood posts separates the entrance from the living-room and leads to one of two alcoves. Walls and paving of stone contrast with the white stucco and relate to the stone exterior.

Casa del Sol Occidente

Careyes Bay, Costa Careyes, Mexico

Like a man-made island resting in a lagoon-like pool over the Pacific, Gianfranco Brignone's sun-shaped guest-house crowns a rocky outcropping at Costa Careyes. Brignone's daughter, photographer Sofia Brignone, designed the landscaping.

n the state of Jalisco along the Mexican coast between Puerta Vallarta and Manzanillo, a contemporary regional beach-house style developed in the 1960s and '70s. Gianfranco Brignone is the wizard responsible for this magic. In the late '60s, this Italian who had spent decades in France fell in love with the hidden coves and bays along Mexico's Pacific coast. He purchased six thousand acres, taming the land on horseback with machete in hand. Having set aside part of the site as a nature preserve to protect the local turtle population, Brignone developed Costa Careyes with a resort hotel, polo club and spectacular houses along the cliffs. These modernist beach-houses feature local colours and *palapa* roofs, as well as clustered pavilions. Built in the manner of the ancient coastal peoples, the individual thatched-roof pavilions have no walls. They reflect an understanding of the setting and of the area's exceptional microclimate; rain usually falls only twenty days each year. The houses merge with the dense vegetation, rocky setting and sandy beaches characteristic of the coast.

Brignone's latest compound of houses, designed in collaboration with French architect Jean-Claude Galibert and local craftsmen, includes twin guest-houses which face one another across the water of a rocky cove, each crowning an outcropping in the Pacific. These houses are sun-shaped, and the rooms open on to the 'lagoon' pool which circulates around both buildings, creating man-made island houses.

One of the guest-houses, Casa del Sol Occidente, has walls which create corridors, link courtyards and form the perimeter around which moat-like swimming pools seem to float. There are few right angles and hard edges. Everything about the house is of Mexican craftsmanship, including the *palapa*, the woodworking and the 'stone carpets' made of local river stones. 'I introduced mixing "magnetite" into the cement. It is found in the sand in some of our beaches, and studies have shown health benefits for prolonging life.' The entrance evokes the concept of the Occident with its fortress-like stone walls.

Casa del Sol Occidente and its neighbour represent Brignone's hope that East and West will one day unite in peace. The houses are connected by the water, and he placed a meteor in the centre of the cove. 'These houses, like all of my constructions, include the four elements: wind, earth, fire as the sun, and water expressed in the pools and views of the ocean,' Brignone says. 'One can place the bed in the centre of the [bed]room, giving a perfect view of the ocean,' he adds. 'I consider my profession as a "picture framer". My houses are the frame and nature is the painting.'

opposite top left Stairs provide a variety of experiences and movement through the house and its corridors. Leading from the entrance hall, stairs to the bedrooms focus on the paved floor depicting the symbol of the sun.

opposite top right Broad curved stairs lead from one level of the entrance hall to another.

opposite left The open *palapa*-covered pavilion at the heart of the house is reached by wide stairs with a sculpted figure standing guard.

opposite right The fortress-like entrance to Casa del Sol Occidente includes a tower with an interior curved stair and deep-set arched windows.

above Casa del Sol Occidente is one of a pair of island-like guest-houses which Brignone built to face each other across the bay of Playa Careyes. 'I like to create "water mirrors,"' he says. The house seems to float in a circular pool which mirrors the ocean. From the central *palapa*-roofed *ramada*, the rooms of the house angle out. Surrounding grounds are terraced and dotted with small *palapa*-roofed garden pavilions.

right Dining in the central pavilion with its open walls and soaring *palapa* roof is like eating out-of-doors. 'The columns are replicas of those from the Cumaean civilization of the Italian peninsula dating to 1000 BC,' says Brignone. The round table is surrounded by pigskin and wicker Equipale chairs.

opposite top The master suite has a raised area for the bed, providing excellent views of the water. 'I try to frame views of the ocean for my guests,' says Brignone. Classical sculptures create dramatic accents while simple furnishings and built-in tables contribute to the carefree resort atmosphere.

opposite Gauzy mosquito netting creates a four-poster effect for the bed in another guest bedroom with curved walls and built-in credenzas.

above Ancient masks and Classical sculptures are displayed above banquettes lined with pillows covered in colourful Mexican fabrics – part of the wealth of local crafts on display in the house.

Water on the Water

Waterside residences which feature outdoor pools bring the essence of their settings right to their very doors. Whatever the style and shape of a pool – and whatever the location of the house it complements – the contrast between the light reflecting off its calm surface and the play and movement of the natural body of water nearby can induce a sense of tranquil amazement. The feeling of floating in a pool beside the sea is almost otherworldly, and to have such an experience in a haven of one's own, surrounded by spectacular views, is simply sublime.

The rustic villas of Antiquity were intended as places of escape and meditation, and that remains unchanged today. Like ancient builders, modern architects experiment with a wide variety of styles, shapes, colours and orientations to maximize the effects they wish to evoke. Whether formally enframed or surrounded by lush vegetation, pools by the waterside provide the ultimate opportunity for contemplative relaxation.

Land-locked Retreats

Surprisingly, definitions which distinguish lakes, ponds, swamps and other bodies of nonoceanic water from one another are not well established. We can say, nonetheless, that ponds are relatively small in comparison to lakes, and that marshes and swamps regularly contain large quantities of grasses, trees or shrubs. Lakes are bodies of slowly moving or standing water which occupy inland basins. They collect water from rivers and cyclical rains and can have shores stretching for miles. Lunar tides are insignificant forces on lakes, whose internal currents are the result of inflows and outflows of water and wind stress. Surface waves cause shore erosion, create beaches and can influence the distribution of shore plants. Standing waves, called seiches, are produced by the wind and by the pressure disturbances which are common and significant to lakes. The usually still water of a reflective lake or pond can virtually suspend time as both lakes and ponds embody notions of collection and reflection.

The economic importance of waterways as communication links has always been enormous, and lake systems, like rivers, play a role in shipping since they often link inland ports with the oceans. Lakes also make a strong aesthetic impact on the adjacent landscape. They enliven it and mirror the trees and foliage. With their varying sizes and forms, lakes and ponds create different atmospheres and inspire a gamut of moods. Claude Monet's lily ponds at Giverny in France became a retreat for the famous Impressionist, in addition to inspiring a stunning series of paintings. The American writer Henry David Thoreau adopted Walden Pond in eastern Massachusetts as his spiritual escape from society. Spirituality in nature is also relevant to the ponds and lakes of Oriental gardens, as at Katsura Palace in Kyoto, where the pond has an intricate winding bank, with many depressions, peninsulas and islands.

Canals or channels provide exquisite textural links between different urban and suburban landscapes. Even though the majority of vernacular buildings along the canals of Bangkok, Amsterdam, Venice, Kyoto and Suzchou are quite bland, their settings impart glamour and character to them all. The canals of Suzchou, a historic Chinese city, offer private moorings and a public garden in which water plays an important role. The medieval 'castle' towns of Japan extended moat protection into a canal system between two rivers at Kanazawa and at Hikone, where the Hachiman moat connects to Lake Biwa. In Thailand, the canal system of Bangkok is fundamental to everyday life, with canal houses raised on pilotis have inviting tropical porches and boat moorings beneath. Britain's nationwide canal system, developed in the 1700s and 1800s, extended the use of existing rivers. Planners reintroduced natural characteristics lost to earlier waterfront development with canal-side towpaths and features that make inland British canal living tasteful and pleasurable.

Floating House

Pond and Wetlands, Nantucket, Massachusetts

New England building traditions influenced Rita and Samuel Robert's vacation house with its gabled clapboard form outlined in white trim. Architect Edward Knowles's design provides outdoor rooms suspended as decks over a pond.

'This is your Taj Mahal,' joked architect Ed Knowles as he presented the model of this New England-style residence surrounded by transparent blue glassine to friends and clients Rita and Samuel Robert on their tenth anniversary. A cedar-clapboard house 'floating' on a Nantucket pond is certainly as reflective and romantic as that palace in India – if slightly more modest.

The Roberts' seven-acre property is surrounded by three hundred acres of conservation land – a rarity on Nantucket today. No-one can build within sight, allowing for uninterrupted views of the horizon and the sunrise and sunset. The pond blends with the site, with local flora, such as bayberry and blue flag iris, planted around the edges. The conservation land includes cranberry bogs and an unusual small area of primeval woods which border the property. They include huge old trees and tupelos which thrive in the wetlands and are glorious in the autumn, when they turn a mahogany colour. 'One of our obsessions was retaining the quality of Nantucket, which is so natural and where nothing looks new or artificial,' explains Sam Robert. 'We gave the house the semblance of age and the traditional regional style by using the cedar clapboards, which quickly turn grey, and including in the design the multiple gables and arched arbours in the gardens.' The arbours show the skill of the boatmaker who built them. Knowles gave the house a Gertrude Jekyll-like croquet lawn on the entrance side, where a curved gravel drive meets the arbour entrance gate. This aspect of the house is designed like a garden pavilion. On the other side, the building changes character and seems like a houseboat with wooden decks barely raised above the water line.

The Roberts chose an inland site for numerous reasons, particularly for ease of maintenance and greater variety in gardening, a favourite pastime of Rita Robert. The pond provides the feeling of living on the water. Weather permitting, the couple take meals outside on the deck; while relaxing on chaises, they feel as if they are aboard a ship. The airy feeling of being on a boat is also apparent inside. Skylights flood the living–dining-room and kitchen with natural light. 'The pond is stocked with koi, or Japanese carp,' explains Rita Robert. 'We started with fifty and now we have closer to five hundred ... besides ... giving us inordinate amounts of pleasure and delighting our grandchildren and guests, they eat the larvae from the mosquitos and eliminate most of them.' The Roberts' grandchildren love the pond; they sit for hours watching the fish. 'There is something zen-like in the movements of the fish, the unbelievable grace with which they just slither through the water,' says Rita Robert. 'And then we go out on our deck and the fish hear our footsteps, and they come out like a flotilla.'

The house is shaped like an L, and the views out of almost all of the windows provide a full reflection of it in the water. At night, particularly when the moon is full, these reflections are extraordinary. The moon and stars are very bright in the clear Nantucket air and shine magically in the water. Changing weather can also be enjoyed, as when the fog arrives in layered banks.

left One wing of the L-shaped house holds the master bedroom suite, which extends out into the pond. A large arched opening with French doors and a lunette leads to a wood deck. The room has a gabled ceiling crossed with wooden beams and illuminatd by a skylight. Furnishings include the four-poster pine bed and tiger-maple chest. Oriental rugs warm the pumpkin-pine floors.

bottom A teak deck chair is framed by the wide French doors focusing on the outdoor deck at one end of the living-room. Inside the gabled space, patterns of light and shadow are created by a skylight which follows the gable ridge, and ever-changing views of Nantucket skies and bird life are visible through the circular clerestory window.

opposite A dining banquette on the kitchen deck is perched over the water. 'We take many of our meals on the deck,' explains Rita Robert, 'and when the Japanese carp hear our footsteps, they surround us with open mouths ready to be fed.' Tupelos and cranberry bogs which surround the Roberts' seven-acre property are part of a three-hundred-acre conservation area which fortuîtously provides the pond site with distant views of the horizon.

Kasteel van's-Gravenwezel

Antwerp, Belgium

A tranquil moat as well as towers with conical and onion-shaped tops create the striking urban presence of Axel and May Vervoordt's medieval castle residence, located near Antwerp and modified in the fifteenth and eighteenth centuries.

Surrounded by a moat and set in a wooded landscape, 's-Gravenwezel Castle is located about six miles north-east of Antwerp. 'The castle, the earliest documented evidence of which dates back to the twelfth century, shows an unusual mixture of fifteenth- and eighteenth-century architecture,' explains Axel Vervoordt, the noted antiques dealer who lives there with his wife, May. History permeates the building. Its medieval porch and eighteenth-century façade, turrets and moat are all familiar to the people of Antwerp.

Vervoordt, who has owned the castle for decades, has given it the character of a comfortable, lived-in noble house. It is his bustling enclave, but shows no signs of being either a showroom or a museum. Every room appears to be lovingly cared for and to carry the Vervoordts' personal imprint. Directly through the entrance hall is the library, which May Vervoordt refers to as their 'evening room'. This is the place to which the couple gravitate to relax at the end of a work-day. This favourite room is filled with a constantly changing collection of fine works of art and furniture. 'Our interest in architecture is reflected in our love of architectural furniture and masterpieces,' says Axel Vervoordt. Cushions covered with Oriental carpeting give the room a casual atmosphere; the Vervoordts' hunting dog usually joins them in the library on his own cushion before the fireplace. One wall of bookshelves displays a pair of anatomical engravings, scaled plaster casts from an artist's studio and wooden armatures, old books, marquetry boxes and spheres made from rock crystal,

wood and marble. Oriental pieces include a Korean bronze vase, Thai and Chinese celadon bowls, Chou-Dynasty jades and stone landscapes.

Each of the castle's tall, rectangular, mullioned windows looks out towards the balustraded terraces and stairs or directly towards the moat, which is filled with lotus during the spring and summer and with ducks and swans year-round. Interior shutters frame many of the views, although some windows in the main rooms are draped with velvet or billowing waterfall-satin draperies. The orangery, where the staff eat lunch, has especially tall windows which provide excellent water views. On a practical note, they are used to hoist in objects, furniture and even boiserie and antique parquet floors for the ever-changing collection.

'In the ideal house, a symbiotic relationship develops between architecture and its dwellers by means of the furniture and objects in it,' says Axel Vervoordt. 'A man's house is to be his favourite place of being, a privileged site with myriad paths he can walk, in an effort to rediscover himself. There has also to be an essential balance between nature and architecture. Windows thus become paintings and create a perspective, an opening on to new possibilities.' Axel Vervoordt's corner study has numerous windows looking out to the water view. It is a charming, cozy space despite its lofty ceilings and practically bare eighteenth-century parquet floor. A fireplace provides warmth. 'Living near the water gives a feeling of security, of living protected on an island, like being on an eternal boat,' says Vervoordt of his fairy-tale castle.

above The tall windows of the corner study look out to the terrace and the broad moat. The wood panelling, parquet floors and marble fireplace represent the Régence-style adaptation of the medieval structure by Jan-Pieter van Baurscheit Jr. The room is furnished with an early nineteenth-century ebony partner's desk.

left While Vervoordt has created a gracious setting for antiques and art, each space is comfortably lived in. One room displays the castle's simpler medieval heritage with a wooden plank floor, exposed-beam ceiling and plain fireplace. The contemporary bronze sculpture is by Lucio Fontana.

right Billowy waterfall-satin draperies of the dining-room's tall, square-mullioned window face a balustraded terrace and the moat, which is filled with lotus during the spring and summer, and with ducks and swans year-round. Like a still-life painting with a waterscape background, an array of seventeenth-century Ming blue-and-white porcelains are displayed on the marble-topped Louis XIV side table.

Boathouse Logic

Cross Lake, Shreveport, Louisiana

Mahogany trim and prow-like windows are perfect for a house docked like a ship on a lake peninsula where regional traditions and works by Palladio and Frank Lloyd Wright inspired Christopher Coe's design for Sherrie and James Lillich.

Architect Christopher Coe refers to his design for this Louisiana lake house as the type of country house described by Andrea Palladio, even quoting the Italian Renaissance architect on the subject of the ideal villa.

'The Lillichs [his patrons in this instance] share an avid interest in architecture, and they desired a unique contemporary residence, yet one based on sound principles of traditional architecture ... they cited diverse examples such as Louisiana plantations, houses in the Caribbean and Greek islands and those designed by Frank Lloyd Wright and Palladio,' Coe says. Symmetry, the gable forms and the white stucco are traditional elements and give the three-part house a Mediterranean feeling. However, the handling of the forms and their details are thoroughly contemporary. Coe wanted to give the house a family-orientated feeling but keep it functional for entertaining, while his patrons wanted it to be orientated towards the lake and designed to maximize the use of natural light. 'We wanted to see as much of the water as possible, and Chris came up with this plan, which includes the guest-house and boathouse and frames the view. From almost anywhere in the main house we can see the water,' explains Sherrie Lillich.

At the lake's edge are a pair of small two-storey, gabled pavilion-houses on either side of the swimming pool and directly on axis with the main house. This is the tranquil view which the Lillichs have of the lake. From the entrance, visitors can see up a long entrance drive, straight through the central portion of the main house – the double-height entrance and living-room –

to the continuous reflections of the lap pool and the lake. Another delightful vista of the lake is seen through the lengthy gable-covered walkway connecting the circular motor-court entrance to a pair of contiguous garages. 'The two-storey boathouse and guest-house straddle the axis and sit on the lake's edge,' Coe says. Considering the formal symmetry of the compound, the pair of houses by the lake may be compared to wings of the main house forming a U-shaped courtyard. The main house is a symmetrical H-plan structure, fully glazed at both front and rear of the central volume.

'We love to go out on the deck just to watch the birds and to be close to the water,' says James Lillich. The protected cove attracts birds of many kinds. Sherrie Lillich enthusiastically describes the wildlife with which she and her family share the water location: 'We see mallards, and quite a variety of different types of ducks, which occasionally come across our yard and get in our swimming pool. Cormorants nest up in the trees right across from us. They come in at dusk, one by one, and they all light on a different branch. They are so white that they shine against the green trees. Also, we have one variety of duck that comes in the late fall by the thousands.' One of the great recreational advantages of the Lillich house is the water-skiing. 'In five minutes, we can be out skiing on the lake,' says James Lillich.

Due to its lake-side site, this house is a practical, year-round home and vacation home in one. And like the ideal Palladian villa, it captures the Renaissance thinker's dictum that a house should provide 'food for mind and body ... to restore and to comfort'.

opposite The architect planned the boathouse and guest-house to frame views of the lake, and, from the living-room catwalk, the guest-house is seen on one side of the pool. Window walls and continuous French limestone paving unite the interior with the pool terrace.

top left The slate-roofed, gabled boathouse sits on the lake's edge where the pool mimics the lake's tranquil reflections. Dan Kiley designed the landscape to merge with the natural setting, including the moss-draped, submerged cypress trees. 'The cypresses out in the water change colours with the seasons,' says Sherrie Lillich.

centre left Following the long axis of the house, the pool is also orientated towards the lake, and the rear façade captures maximum views and natural light through the central glazed bay and the glass terrace doors of the wings.

below left Glimpses of the lake can be seen at the front of the house and through the central glazed portion of the double-height entrance. The symmetrical gabled forms and white stucco are traditional elements which give the house a contemporary Mediterranean feeling with touches of colour from the mahogany window and door trim and copper gutters.

above The catwalk and airy spaces continue the house's ship allusions into the living-room. Finnish materials include steel handrails; mahogany doors, windows and cabinetry; beige limestone paving; and fabric-wrapped acoustical ceilings. Kathryn Hampton Coe co-ordinated the interiors with the Lillichs' collection of modern furniture and reproductions of nineteenth- and twentieth-century classics.

Tower Tree House

Lake Naivasha, Nairobi, Kenya

Lake Naivasha near Nairobi has many varieties of birds, including the rare fish eagle. Among its yellow fever trees is the tapering octagonal tower built by Michael and Dodo Cunningham-Reid as an exotic retreat on their five-hundred-acre game preserve.

The lake-shore residents of Lake Naivasha in Kenya are colobus monkeys, cheetahs, giraffes, impalas and zebras. They, and a number of hippos and donkeys, graze along the shores, and the rare fish eagle has given the lake a distinguished reputation. All these animals and birds share their habitat with Dodo and Michael Cunningham-Reid.

The lake is part of the former Delamere estate. As the stepson of Tom, Lord Delamere, Michael Cunningham-Reid lived nearby during his teenage years. He fell in love with the landscape, and he and Dodo later purchased five hundred acres of the estate as a game preserve and vacation retreat.

'I planned our house as a folly because the fantastic nature of the setting commands it,' says Dodo Cuningham-Reid. 'Anything else would have looked too ordinary.' The folly's wood siding and octagonal shape reflect the German-born Dodo's Nordic background. Yellow fever trees, common to the Rift Valley lakes, are as tall as the tower and have similar colouring; in fact, they inspired its height, colour and plan. The tower, roofed in copper and clad in Kenyan cypress siding, is wide on the lower two levels to provide living and dining spaces, and narrower at the top for bedrooms, studies and viewing eyries.

Watching the lake and its banks allows innumerable sightings of local wildlife. 'My favourite rooms are the seventh-floor study and the first-floor drawing-room,' says Dodo Cunningham-Reid. 'Both face the lake, the mountains and the endless skies.' The charming interior furnishings and fine art were all selected by her; some are European, while other items were made in Nairobi. 'Many of the antiques, including the living-room's Gothic Revival table, came from the estate of my mother, Mary, Lady Delamere,' says Michael Cunningham-Reid.

The Cunningham-Reids initially intended to use the folly as a vacation retreat. They invited friends who then wanted to share the unique experience with other friends. Finally, the Cunningham-Reids were convinced to open the Tower at Lake Naivasha as an élite bed and breakfast. In addition to staying in the wonderful rooms with their entrancing views, guests enjoy lunch on the lawn and on the first-floor terrace, facing the peaceful lake and phenomenal landscape. 'This is by far one of the most beautiful places in the world,' says Dodo Cunningham-Reid. 'Where else do you have giraffes coming out of the bush to greet you at breakfast? Or hippos waking you at dawn? Mist rolls in from the lake at night, and during the rainy season the sky immerses the earth in pink and purple. It's a perfect retreat.'

above The master bedroom on the third floor has a 360-degree terrace view accessible through the square-mullioned glass door. The room is panelled in mahogany which was rubbed with white and yellow paint to lighten the colour, and it is furnished with a French nineteenth-century gilt sleigh bed and writing desk.

opposite Dodo Cunningham-Reid planned the house as a folly to suit the fantastic nature of the setting.

right 'Interior furnishings include furniture from London, antiques from France, and European and local African fabrics,' says Dodo Cunningham-Reid. One corner of the mahogany-panelled library shows built-in bookshelves and glazed double doors. 'Like the living-room, it has panoramic terrace views of the lake, the mountains and the trees.'

Venetian Revival

Lake Worth Lagoon, Palm Beach, Florida

An Addison Cairns Mizner 1920s Venetian palazzo on a Florida lake was recently renovated by designer Howard Slatkin. Built as a vacation cottage, it retains a gondola port, courtyard, pointed-arched openings and trefoil surrounds.

As the residents fish from their courtyard terrace, protected by the wings of the U-shaped plan, they can look out to the shimmering lagoon off Lake Worth near Palm Beach, Florida, which first inspired architect Addison Cairns Mizner to design this Venetian-style palazzo in the mid-1920s. Mizner's 'cottages' were calculated to catapult their owners into the highest levels of society, and this house did not disappoint. Casa di Leoni took on the regal character of St Mark's in Venice. A grand winged lion graces the tympanum above the entrance door in honour of the house's original owner, Leonard 'Leo' Thomas.

Mizner, the originator of the Palm Beach Style, created atmospheres redolent of deteriorating magnificence in order to establish Old-World lineage for the newly rich. To achieve the patina of age immediately, he used Florida pecky cypress, a pitted wood commonly employed for pilings and fence posts, and had his workmen take sledgehammers to the stone mantels, balustrades and carvings. He also sent them up and down the concrete stairs in hobnailed boots to simulate years of wear. Even though the Mizneresque atmosphere lingers at Casa di Leoni, the house has recently been preserved and enhanced in a sympathetic manner by an American businessman with the help of interior designer Howard Slatkin.

Designed in typical Mizner fashion as a small recreational cottage with a gondola port, the house has several levels of roofs, windows, gardens and terraces. Throughout, there are Venetian arched openings, mudéjar woodwork ceilings, Moorish lanterns and grillwork. Unlike the traditional Venetian house, but like other Mizner houses, Casa di Leoni follows a traditional Spanish U-shaped hacienda plan to facilitate cross ventilation. On the ground floor, a pool salon extends off to one side, and many tall, slender, arched doors open the rooms of the main salon and dining-room to views of the lagoon and lake. On the first floor, the corner master bedroom has balustraded lake views on two sides.

Mizner often blended Spanish, Moorish and Italian elements, and particularly liked the Venetian style because it combined Gothic with Baroque forms. Many of the original architectural details at Casa di Leoni are intact. Howard Slatkin enhanced the Mediterranean mood by installing a wall fountain in the courtyard and paving the same space with native coquina stone. He elaborated further on the Venetian theme by adding custom trim, passementerie – including custom-designed tassels and tie-backs – and an Arabic ceiling. Now a waterside hideaway for a young family, Casa di Leoni is a playful folly where home and furnishings have the look and feel of centuries of faded grandeur.

above The living-room displays the rich, multi-patterned style of the interiors which Howard Slatkin created for the American businessman who hired him to bring the house back from the brink of disrepair. For Slatkin's work rebuilding the balconies and restoring the French doors which open to the courtyard, the Preservation Foundation of Palm Beach gave the house the Ballinger Award in 1995.

left Floor-to-ceiling French doors open the dining-room to the terrace and to the view of the lagoon. Unlike Mizner's original design, Slatkin tented the dining-room, hiding the original ceiling.

opposite A corner of the library reveals Slatkin's layer-on-layer of fabric patterning and faux fur prints, which are unlike Mizner's flamboyant style, but are a new interpretation of Mizneresque Floridian style.

The Gardens of Versailles

Nineteenth-Century Decoration

GERE   THE ART OF THE INTERIOR   ABRAMS

Tenth-Century Treasure

Lake Orta, San Giulio, Italy

Formerly a tavern, post stop and lodge, a slate-roof stone cottage from 962 AD retains a fragment of its grounds, which originally extended to Lake Orta. It has been renovated as a home by architect Mario Tedeschi.

Under a pergola overgrown with strawberry grapes, the outdoor dining table of an ancient structure looks out to the tiny island of San Giulio, which arises like a fantasy out of the dark blue waters of Lake Orta in the north of Italy. The house was originally built as a civic structure a thousand years ago. Now it is embued with the history of the area. Like the other remaining ancient structures in the region, it represents the simple local architecture constructed during the Middle Ages.

The building was originally the place where villagers greeted the arrival of the post. Few such surviving structures are of such fine design and materials. The house has a typical large horse stall covered by a beautiful stone vault (now the garage), and the ground floor – formerly the tavern and rest stop – has a grand stone fireplace reconstructed from original stones.

From the exterior, the house's distinguishing element is the high, pitched slate roof, evidence of Nordic influence. The building, which sits in story-book fashion on a verdant slope overlooking the lake, was sensitively renovated by architect Mario Tedeschi, who collaborated with landscape architect Elena Balsari Berrone. Today, other houses impinge on the original emerald grounds which terraced down to the lake-shore unobstructed, but the site remains ample.

Addressing issues of convenience and modern accommodation, Tedeschi left the original outer walls and modified the interior walls as little as possible. Such new elements as two columns of local granite are tasteful and harmonious. Inspired by historic methods and plans, the redistribution of the spaces is in keeping with the sequences and ambience of the original structure. Numerous craftspeople worked on the renovation.

The living-room is filled with art and antiques. Hanging from the old woodwork are fragments of a tapestry by Tino Bellini, and beside the stone fireplace is a painting by Federica Marangoni. The room features a grand pentagonal table from Lombardy, dating from the end of the sixteenth century. Next to the window, some glass spheres and a French glass lamp sparkle in the reflected light, which changes according to the season.

While the outdoor dining-room faces the lake, the interior one is painted to match the colours of nature – lime, ochre, sage and ivory. The two granite columns stand next to two wooden sculptures of Mongolian horses from the seventeenth century. In the master bedroom, characterized by the original woodwork, an Empire-period sleigh bed from Naples is set at an angle. Representing the owners' passion for history, the furnishings and objects are embraced by the rustic, hand-crafted structure – the timber posts, rafters and beams, and the reconstructed slate roof. Throughout the interiors, the walls are animated by antique tapestries, which add warmth, colour and texture. Windows open the medieval structure to the garden and the lake view.

opposite above Original to the medieval building, the low beamed ceiling and reconstructed stone fireplace enhance the antique character of the living-room. Bookshelves and the low table piled with books, as well as the objects of art and antiquity, display the interests of the residents. The preservation and renovation of the structure were overseen by the Erbea e Montani di Orta San Giulio foundation.

opposite left A modern brick-paved gallery-style kitchen has been inserted into one of the ground-floor spaces of the medieval structure.

opposite right One corner of the gabled attic holds a bath and dressing room. The numerous craftspeople who worked on the house include woodworker Luigi Pozzi di Cantù and ironworkers Ruga and Piralli di Gazzano.

above Grapevines frame the view of the village on the tiny island of San Giulio which rises like an ancient vision out of Lake Orta. The vine-covered pergola shades the outdoor dining table.

right Dining-room walls painted lime, ochre, sage and ivory match the colours of nature, as seen through the arched windows. The inclusion of the local grey granite column was inspired by the original plans. The Mongolian horse is from the seventeenth century.

below right A new stairway is juxtaposed with the ancient gabled roof. The renovating architect accommodated contemporary needs while respecting the structure. In the stair hall, the redistributed spaces are in keeping with the sequences of the ancient building.

opposite An Empire-period sleigh bed from Naples dominates the master bedroom, where the original ceiling timbers and wall surfaces are preserved.

Gazebos and Follies

Gazebos and belvederes most commonly provide commanding vistas of the water. These free-standing structures with their completely open sides or multiplicity of windows provide 360-degree views. It is like being on the open water amongst shifting breezes, scents and the play of sun- or moonlight. Of no practical use, gazebos and belvederes simply exist for pleasure. These are places for observation, meditation, entertainment – maybe even dancing and romancing – all in view of the water.

Waterside follies, unlike gazebos, are frequently inward-looking or open to the view in a limited, carefully considered way. They tend to be contemplative, even melancholy spaces, intended for deep thought and reflection, or for reading or writing, with the water nearby providing gentle hints of inspiration, perhaps less seen than heard. Often miniaturized or deliberately playful renderings of antiquated or vernacular building forms, follies can provide delightful, eccentric accents to waterside properties.

Photography Credits

James Alinder: 13

Michel Arnaud: 180–83

Robert Emmett Bright: 20–25, 58–59 (TOP RIGHT), 93 (RIGHT and BOTTOM), 124–29, 140–45, 161 (BOTTOM RIGHT and BOTTOM MIDDLE), 184–89

Sofia Brignone: 6–7, 93 (TOP RIGHT), 154–59, 160 (TOP LEFT)

Steven Brooke: 58 (TOP LEFT), 62–65, 172–75, 191 (RIGHT)

Tim Buchman: 121 (BOTTOM RIGHT)

Luis Casals: 150–53

Mario Ciampi: 66–67, 68 (TOP RIGHT, BOTTOM LEFT and BOTTOM RIGHT), 69

Dariascagliala & Sijnbrakkee: 120 (BOTTOM LEFT)

Scott Francis/ESTO: 120–21 (BOTTOM MIDDLE), 121 (TOP RIGHT)

Mistumasa Fujitsuka: 2

Jeff Goldberg/ESTO: 60–61, 74–79, 120 (TOP LEFT), 130–33, 160 (BOTTOM LEFT), 191 (TOP), 190–91 (BOTTOM RIGHT)

Heidi Grassley: 11, 58–59 (BOTTOM LEFT), 70–73, 80–83, 92 (BOTTOM MIDDLE and BOTTOM LEFT), 96–101, 120–21 (TOP RIGHT), 164–67, 190–91 (TOP RIGHT)

Kees Hageman: 170–71

Alexander Hansen: 40–43, 160–61 (BOTTOM RIGHT)

Stephen W. Harby: 14, 17, 191 (BOTTOM)

Thomas A. Heinz: 1

Michael Jensen: 88–91, 92–93 (TOP RIGHT)

Lourdes Legorreta: 116–19

Bertrand Limbour: 168–69

Mike Moore: 26–29

Jonathan Pilkington: 162–63, 176–79, 190 (BOTTOM LEFT)

Antonio Quaresma: 112 (BOTTOM RIGHT)

João Ribeiro/Editora AÇÕA Publicações LTDA: 110–11, 112 (TOP), 113–15

Willy Rizzo: 44–47

John C. Russell: 102–5

Deidi von Schaewen: 18–19, 30–33, 34–39, 48–53, 54–57, 58 (LEFT), 59 (TOP RIGHT, RIGHT and BOTTOM), 84–87, 121 (TOP MIDDLE), 134–39, 160–61 (TOP RIGHT), 161 (TOP RIGHT), 190 (TOP LEFT)

Hisao Suzuki: 68 (TOP LEFT)

Christopher Simon Sykes: 94–95, 106–9

Marie-Hélène Villierme: 122–23, 146–49

Michael Webb: 6 (LEFT), 92 (TOP LEFT)